THE AUTHORS

A. J. Lerro, Assistant Professor of Finance at Virginia Polytechnic Institute, Blacksburg, Virginia, received his Ph. D. from the University of Alabama in 1964. Professor Lerro, a member of several professional finance and economic associations, has written articles in finance and business economics.

C. B. Swayne, Jr., a registered investment advisor graduated from Virginia Polytechnic Institute with degrees in Mechanical Engineering and Business Administration. He has taught at Radford College for Women and Virginia Polytechnic Institute. In addition, he has been employed with the Eastman Kodak Co. Currently, Mr. Swayne is serving as Captain in the U. S. Army.

SELECTION OF SECURITIES:

Technical Analysis
of
Stock Market Prices

SELECTION OF SECURITIES:
Technical Analysis
of
Stock Market Prices

Anthony J. Lerro

Charles B. Swayne, Jr.

D. H. MARK PUBLISHING COMPANY
BRAINTREE, MASSACHUSETTS

46665

Printed in the United States of America

Library of Congress Catalog Card Number: 73-100575

TO OUR PARENTS

Preface

The selection of securities is approached by two basic avenues: the fundamental or intrinsic value method, and technical analysis. The former is usually offered on the undergraduate level. The latter approach is often left for the individual to learn in his spare time, although brokerage firms do attempt to train their employees, especially those newly hired, in the basic elements of technical analysis.

It is obvious that a very serious gap exists between career-oriented brokers and other individuals who eventually join the ranks of the investing public. The authors believe that a thorough presentation of technical analysis can help to bridge this gap.

Since a plethora of information is available relating to the fundamental approach to security analysis, we will not consider its numerous aspects. The reader, however, is urged to familiarize himself with its basic tenets as presented in the classic, *Security Analysis,* by Graham, Dodd, and Cottle.

This book is divided into two major parts. Part I introduces the simplest form of charting – the bar chart. Part II emphasizes the point and figure approach. The underlying principles applicable to bar charting carry over to the point and figure method, but the technique is somewhat different.

We believe that the book is unique in combining the approaches to both schools in a single volume. In addition, an ample number of actual examples are presented for reference purposes.

Although it would be impossible to acknowledge the guidance and counsel of those many colleagues who assisted us, we are especially grateful to *TRENDLINE* for permission to use their charts. This service greatly reduced the amount of time required in preparing the text material. In addition, we are indebted to the Virginia Polytechnic

Institute librarians, especially Miss Betty D. Davis, who uncovered many references cited in the book.

We urge serious chartists to read other relevant material. In particular we suggest Robert D. Edwards and John Magee, *Technical Analysis of Stock Trends*; William L. Jiler, *How Charts Can Help You in the Stock Market*; A. H. Wheelan, *Study Helps in Point and Figure Technique* and *The Chartcraft Method of Point and Figure Trading*. In addition Joseph E. Granville's *New Key to Stock Market Profits* and his *A Strategy of Daily Stock Market Timing for Maximum Profit* deserve mention. Other references presented in this book provide excellent reading material for the trader.

Errors and omissions are clearly our responsibility. It is our hope that serious followers of technical analysis will offer additional suggestions for improving the subject matter.

Dr. A. J. Lerro
C. B. Swayne, Jr.

Contents

PART I ANALYSIS OF BAR CHARTS

PART II ANALYSIS OF POINT AND FIGURE CHARTS

PART I

Analysis of Bar Charts

THIS SECTION of the book is devoted to the most widely used approach to charting – namely bar charting. Many of the basic principles which apply to bar charting also form the basis to the point and figure method described in Part II.

It is suggested that the reader carefully study the accompanying charts, which relate to the real world of charting, as a means of becoming aware of and involved with the factors comprising technical analysis.

1

Scope and Nature of Investments and Technical Analysis

BACKGROUND

An investment represents the ownership of property, real or personal, with the intention of gain. This definition is quite broad and is not restricted to the ownership of securities. That is, a person may purchase land as a means of realizing potential future profit. Such a transaction, of course, involves real property. On the other hand, the commitment of funds for securities represents an exchange of money for personal property.

In fact, the term "ownership" is used rather loosely because in many cases money may be borrowed, in whole or in part, in order to purchase a particular type and quantity of asset.

From a narrow point of view, we may define an investment as the ownership of corporate securities in the form of either common stock, preferred stock, or bonds.

The term "investment" may be subject to considerable criticism at this juncture. Graham, Dodd, and Cottle associate a security investment with "safety of principal."[1] For our purposes the term "investment" is not restricted to quality, although technical analysis may be limited to include only the study of high-grade common stocks. That is, a person may limit the selection of common stocks for charting to those which fall into the classification of "A+," "A," or "A-," as established by Standard and Poor's or similar rating services. Certainly, quality is not to be completely ignored, since those basic factors which create

[1] Benjamin Graham, David Dodd, and Sidney Cottle, *Security Analysis* (4th ed.: New York: McGraw-Hill Book Company, 1962), p. 49.

quality – earnings,   dividends,   and   the   like – do   affect   price
movements.

TECHNICAL ANALYSIS DEFINED

Technical analysis may be defined as the art of studying, in
graphic form, the internal performance or action of stocks.[2] The
statistical factors which are the all-important technical elements making
up the chart or picture are: market-price movements; volume, breadth
and depth indicators; and short position, to name a few. These factors
will be clarified as we move along.

The underlying philosophy of technical analysis is the prompt
recognition of trends or formations. Once plotted, trends display
certain characteristics or clues which are then interpreted as
information useful to the chartists. In effect the chartist is attempting
to follow the psychological actions of numerous buyers and sellers in
the market place. By definition psychology is concerned with the study
of behavior.[3] The market place becomes the center where various
behaviorial patterns are reflected. Whether the personal motivation is
rational or irrational is immaterial; we are interested only in measuring
the verdict relative to the price movement of securities. In short, the
market place discounts all news, excluding acts of God.[4]

The interplay of buying and selling is the key to chart patterns.
Specifically, when there are more buyers than sellers, then (applying
simple economic logic), the stock can be acquired only by bidding up
the price; a bullish signal to the chartist. If selling predominates, buyers
are willing to purchase only at a price lower than the going market; a
bearish market prevails. Such attitudes are readily observable as the
chartist registers the respective price changes.

Since charting has a large following, one might look upon its
technical aspect as an attempt to locate favorably situated stocks before
the general public participates in them. Above all else, chart forecasting
is an attempt to buy or sell before a significant change occurs in public
opinion.

---

[2]Some people refer to charting as a "science" or a "quasi-science"; however, the
writers believe otherwise. See, for example, John Brooks, "Onward and Upward
with the Arts," *The New Yorker*, June 23, 1956, p. 42.
[3]Clifford T. Morgan, *Introduction to Psychology* (New York: McGraw-Hill Book
Company, 1956), pp. 3–4.
[4]Robert Rhea, *The Dow Theory* (New York: Vail-Ballou Press, Inc., 1959), p. 12.

Perhaps Lord Keynes inadvertently described the chartist philosophy in the simplest language when he noted that:

> . . . newspaper competitors . . . have to pick out the six prettiest faces from a hundred photographs . . . each competitor [chooses] those which he thinks likeliest to catch the fancy of other competitors, all of whom are looking at the problem from the same point of view.[5]

Thus, the chartist, like a newspaperman, is trying to locate via technical analysis those stocks — pretty girls — which he believes will win the contest — appreciate the most in price. In short, the technical approach is just another basis for anticipating future price movements, with one exception: that it is more direct in its application than the intrinsic value method.

The obvious danger in charting lies in the interpretation of price movements. At this juncture a word of caution is in order. Charting can and does present signals which can be disastrous to the anxious investor. For this reason it is important to remember that chart analysis is not an infallible approach for predicting stock prices. A reckless excursion beyond posted speed limits is quite often expensive; the same pitfalls await those who fail to exercise prudence and judgment in the realm of charting.

[5] John Maynard Keynes, *The General Theory of Employment, Interest and Money* (New York: Harcourt, Brace and Co., 1936), p. 156.

2

Philosophy of Market Trends

THE DOW THEORY

Wall Street historians and experts attribute the origin of charting to the Dow Theory, which is concerned with measuring the general trend of stock market price movements. Particular attention is accorded the Dow-Jones Industrial Average and the Dow-Jones Rail Average. Together these two components form the backbone of chart analysis.

PRINCIPLES RELATING TO THE DOW THEORY

Stocks exhibit strong tendencies to move as a group, although some, of course, rise faster then others. When optimism abounds, the trend of stock prices is upward; as pessimism enters the market place stock prices begin to decline. Emphasis among Dow theorists is on the "togetherness" of price movements.

Relying upon the psychology of "togetherness," these theorists observe three types of price trends – primary, secondary or intermediate, and minor.

As a matter of convenience, Dow theorists frequently compare price trend movements to the action of the sea.[1] First there are "tides," which refer to primary trends. "Waves" pertain to intermediate steps,

[1] For an elaboration of the Dow Theory, see William P. Hamilton, *The Stock Market Barometer* (New York: Harper and Brothers, Publishers, 1922), particularly Chapters V, V111.

and "ripples" identify minor fluctuations. Clearly investors should ride the major trends. But how are these situations identified on charts?

Several clues are available. Primary trends are characterized by broad, up and down price swings which last from cycle to cycle. The over-all phase may span several years. On a chart, the zig-zagging line continues to reach higher and higher levels in a primary upward trend. The intermediate or secondary movements are corrections which cause a temporary pause in the major trend. Minor trends are very small corrections or dips, lasting perhaps for a week or so.

TREND DICHOTOMY

The primary upturn is similar to the operation of a three-speed transmission. The low gear represents an accumulation period. At this speed business conditions are at their worst. Characteristically, the daily volume is light; corporate earnings reports are gloomy; interest rates are below those of earlier periods. At such a time the Dow-Jones Industrial Average tends to be "flat." That is, it neither rises nor falls by many points.

Technically speaking, the market has "bottomed out." Knowledgeable investors, sensing this economic condition, begin to "accumulate" high-quality stocks for the long pull. In all probability these early purchases are made on a full cash basis, not on margin. Minor rallies begin and the Dow-Jones averages begin to creep slowly upward.

A movement into second gear brings other investors back into the market. This group has been inactive, waiting on the sidelines for positive improvements in the economic indicators. At this point, economic reports, while somewhat pessimistic, begin to forecast better conditions. Corporations are beginning to recall unemployed workers. Financial newspapers are reporting increased capital expenditure plans among corporations. Such events are observable when there is a marked tendency for the volume of stock trading to increase in tempo.

In high gear it is obvious that business conditions are good; financial news is especially bright. By this time a firm's upward trend in market prices can be observed. Margin trading is enjoying renewed vigor. Spectacular price swings are increasingly frequent. Market prices of the very poorest companies, "cats" and "dogs," are performing remarkably well but on an unwarranted basis. If the *Wall Street Journal* were opened to the bond tables, one would find the yields there high relative to common stock yields. At this latter stage market volume is soaring; however, high-quality stocks show signs of losing their forward thrust. In other words, there are more investors supplying these shares than there are buyers. Another sign of general weakness is the preponderance of new stock issues and secondary offerings.

In the last analysis, intelligent investors are beginning to prefer the sidelines as they start to notice that rallies are not being sustained for long periods of time. The more professional traders, instead of choosing inactivity, may begin to initiate short selling in the more vulnerable types of stocks, particularly those labeled as high flyers or performance stocks. Of course, economic conditions are such that interest rates have risen. The public is beginning to pay more attention to its ability to absorb further debt. The knowledgeable investor sees that the automobile is running out of gas, albeit at the top of a hill; fortunately, he can coast downhill. On the other hand, panic overcomes the less experienced investor as the Dow-Jones Industrial Average declines dramatically on very high volume. Those who bought on margin begin to sell in order to minimize losses.

It is difficult to pin-point any single item as causing the car to run out of gas. While the market rises to new highs, occasional economic and fincancial reports usually signal several apparent weak spots in the business world. Such news may concern large inventories in steel, declining machine tool orders, signs of tightening credit, dealer inability to sell automobiles, or a large firm announcing poor quarterly earnings. In the end the accumulation of unfavorable news finally explodes as a result, perhaps, of General Motors announcing a cut-back in auto production. In other words, the market has become nervous from hearing poor news and finally collapses from fatigue.

After a while the market will probably experience a strong rally, after which prices will drift sideways. But this is a momentary pause and finally market prices plunge into their last phase. At this point those who bought late and suffered through the initial decline begin to sell their holdings. Others who purchased stocks during the most recent secondary rally join the ranks of the distressed sellers. Characteristically the final deterioration occurs as discouraging financial news abounds. With a few more minor adjustments on the down side the bottom is finally reached. Many individual issues are in an oversold condition; that is, the current price is well below what is warranted even at recessionary levels. Generally, bargin hunters are quick to observe this disparity and absorb such issues on minor price dips.

DOW-JONES CORRELATION

According to the Dow theorist, the Dow-Jones Industrial Average must be confirmed by a similar movement in the Dow-Jones Rail Average before any conclusion can be reached regarding trend analysis.[2] Usually both averages tend to move together; however, there are instances in which a lag exists for several days, weeks, or perhaps a month. In this latter case, the investor must force himself to be patient until confirmation occurs.

One can maintain that, since railroads do not play as important a role in our economy as in former years, the rail averages are unimportant relative to trend analysis. This line of reasoning may be defended, but since a large number of seasoned chartists look for this psychological guideline as a confidence index, it behooves the neophyte to follow the same pattern of action.[3]

[2] Hamilton, op. cit., pp. 185–187. See also Rhea, The Dow Theory, op. cit., pp. 68–74.

[3] Proof that confirmation of the railroad average is still important may be seen in the following comment: "The Dow-Jones rail average continues to be a fly in the technicians' ointment because it has failed so far to match, or confirm last month's advance of the industrial average." See Charles J. Alia, "A breast of the Market," Wall Street Journal October 9, 1967, p. 31.

3

Bar Charting Procedure

Just as accounting is an important tool for the fundamentalist, charting serves as the working tool for the technician. Charts may take a variety of forms depending upon the intentions of the trader. Some professionals may prefer to make monthly recordings for future reference. Others may consider weekly recordings. Lastly, stocks of current interest are plotted on a daily basis. The advantage of such a detailed chart is that the technician can readily observe certain signals which might not be detected as rapidly on a weekly or monthly grid.

BAR CHART CONSTRUCTION

A typical simplified bar chart involves the use of arithmetical graph paper. The vertical axis represents price, while the horizontal scale pertains to the time span — day, week, or month. In constructing a daily vertical bar chart, the necessary information for plotting tl. chart is obtained from the stock market table which appears in the daily newspaper. A dot is entered on the graph paper to indicate the highest price reported and another dot to mark the lowest price for that day. A vertical line connecting these two points represents the high and low price reached for that particular day. A short tick or horizontal crossline is added to mark the closing price. For example, a stock trading on April 4, 1967, between a range of $27 and $30, with a closing price of $29, will appear in the manner shown in Figure 1.

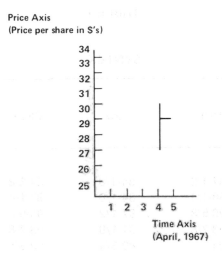

Price Axis
(Price per share in $'s)

Time Axis
(April, 1967)

FIGURE 1. BAR CHART

A careful technician will reserve sufficient space at the bottom of the respective bar chart to plot the volume of activity traded in that stock each day. This is shown by drawing a vertical line extending upward from the horizontal base line on the existing bar chart to match the appropriate figure indicated on the vertical scale. Volume is published daily in hundreds of shares and is easily plotted.

For purposes of clarity, let us examine a typical charting period from April 3, 1967 to April 28, 1967. The stock data in Table 1 indicates the data necessary for charting Syntex (Figure 2).

Some analysts do not chart the daily high and low prices, but only the daily closing price. This simplifies the process but overlooks penetrations into new high and low areas. One must bear in mind that while a wide variety of short cuts are available for diagnosing the action of stocks, proper charting on a daily basis is the most effective method of spotting the course of price movements. Just as a nurse punctually charts a patient's fever in order to detect significant changes in his condition, the trader should frequently evaluate the continuously changing price conditions of key stocks. It is equally important to chart daily volume activity as a clue in determining investor interest.

SELECTION OF SECURITIES

TABLE 1

SYNTEX

Date	High	Low	Close	Volume Traded
April				
3	87-1/2	84-1/8	84-3/8	21,800
4	88-1/4	84-1/8	87-1/4	35,300
5	90-5/8	87-1/2	90-5/8	28,600
6	93-7/8	91-1/8	93-7/8	69,600
7	94	89-3/4	89-3/4	39,100
10	89	86-1/8	87-1/2	39,200
11	90	88-1/4	89-3/8	28,600
12	91-3/4	88-5/8	89-1/8	36,100
13	93-5/8	89-1/4	93-1/4	52,500
14	95	92-5/8	93-1/2	61,900
17	97-1/4	94-1/2	97-1/8	80,200
18	99	96-3/8	98-1/2	73,800
19	97-1/8	95-5/8	95-7/8	50,900
20	97-7/8	95	97-7/8	32,000
21	101-7/8	98-1/4	101-1/2	77,400
24	102-3/4	99-1/8	100-3/8	43,000
25	105	99-1/2	104-7/8	48,400
26	105-3/8	102-1/4	102-3/8	38,600
27	104-5/8	102-3/8	104	26,600
28	105	102-1/2	102-3/4	15,900

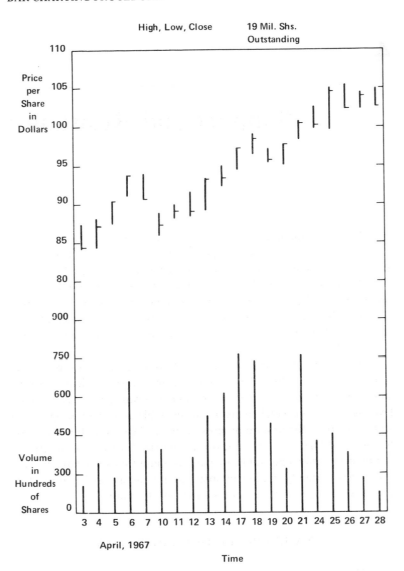

FIGURE 2. SYNTEX

4

Support and Resistance

Two key factors to technical analysts are the "support" and "resistance" levels. The importance of these terms cannot be stressed enough; they describe fundamental tools for buying and selling action.

An individual must learn the rules of the game before becoming a bridge player. Otherwise the match becomes one of extreme tension and anguish. This situation is analogous to that of the trader. He must make sure that each stock possesses the proper technical factors if he is to enjoy the fruits of his labor.

By definition, support is a barrier to price decline. A support level is a price zone in which there is considerable appeal or demand for the stock. In contrast, resistance is a barrier to advancement. A resistance level is a zone in which there is considerable selling or supplying of stock, deterring the upward progress of price. Attention should be given to the word "barrier" because, while a barrier forms an obstruction, it is not necessarily impossible to pass. A mountain or a large body of water may certainly impose an obstruction to an advancing army, but a properly equipped force can mass a successful assault.

DYNAMICS OF SUPPORT AND RESISTANCE

The basis for support and resistance levels is not difficult to understand once the typical reaction of various traders is analyzed. Let us suppose that a stock has had a very rapid rise from $22 to $32 and at the latter price experiences a considerable amount of selling. The pressure is assumed to be heavy enough to weaken the price structure so that a retreat or correction carries the price to $28. Hoping that the

14

stock will return to the $32 level, the late buyers tend to maintain their position in the stock. Assume that a series of minor rallies pushes prices back to the $30–$32 area but fails to penetrate higher levels. The longer the stock remains in the $30–$32 area, the more disenchanted and depressed the high-price buyers become. Their attitude has changed and they become willing to dispose of their holdings just to break even.

Day-to-day fluctuations in the $30–$32 area establish the trading zone with $32 being the resistance point. On a graph (Figure 3) the sequence of trading portrays a series of sideways moves referred to as a "congestion" or "consolidation" area.

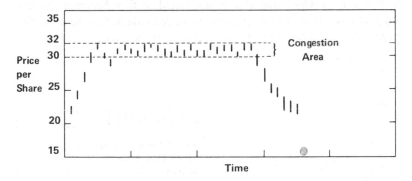

FIGURE 3. CONGESTION MOVEMENT

In the congestion phase there is a constant shifting or churning of stock from buyers who bought at, say $17 to $19, but failed to redeem their shares at the peak price of $32. Other traders who observed the rapid rise now regard minor price dips to $30 as an ideal buy situation. Thus, the latter price forms the support level. Once the old supply overhanging the market is removed from the scene the stock is ready to assault its previous resistance level.

Let us suppose that suppliers are satisfied. This indicates that a strong base is established and any new buying would have to occur at higher bid prices. Consequently, the stock begins to push through its resistance level, perhaps to $37.

In our example the $30–$32 area now becomes the support level. Hence, if our stock began to retreat we would expect renewed buying or increased demand in that area. From where would the new support be derived? For one thing, those who became impatient and discouraged during the consolidation period would wish that they had maintained their former position; they would welcome an opportunity to buy back at the former level. Short sellers would now use any noticeable decline to cover their positions. Also, new traders would consider this level as an attractive buy area.

The crucial point is this: Once a former resistance level is surpassed, it becomes a support level in the event of a decline in price. In other words, the resistance and support have interchangeable roles.

To recapitulate in diagrammatic form (Figure 4): The technician draws a dotted horizontal line to mark the support level at $30-$32. In all probability the price will run into renewed resistance around $37-$40 level. Once this area is penetrated, it then becomes the new support level. It is not our purpose to be redundant, but the seesawing process from resistance to support is frequently ignored.

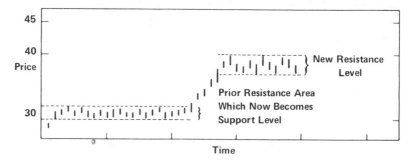

FIGURE 4. SUPPORT AND RESISTANCE AREA

Equally significant is the point that a previous support level may become a resistance level. For instance, assume that our stock rises to $50. Naturally, the old resistance level of $37-$40 is now considered a support area. With a strong bearish trend the stock may drift back to the $30-$32 range before meeting solid support. A rally to the $37-$40 level without penetration on strong volume dubs this area as the new resistance level.

DETERMINING SUPPORT AND RESISTANCE LEVELS

Because of the nature of prices within different price ranges, rapidity of price moves, and volume activity, it is difficult to set a precise standard for determining support and resistance levels.

For a very low-price stock selling at $5 or less, it is most doubtful that a guide will apply, since very few professionals chart this range of prices. At this level of trading most activity stems from tape watchers, semi-boiler room tactics, and grandiose rumors. Moreover, a decline from perhaps $7 to $4 is not usually viewed with alarm, as most uninformed speculators maintain the simple belief that the stock will easily return to its former level. Nothing could be further from the truth, of course. Otherwise the world would be crowded with people relating how their low-price stock made them wealthy.

For most other stocks the "technical rebound rule" tends to work with considerable success. That is, after a stock has experienced a rapid advance or decline, it tends to retrack a third to two-thirds of its original move. Thus, if a stock has swung from $30 to $60 many traders will quickly redeem their stock in order to secure profits. On the decline, bargain hunters look for the opportunity to take a position. Thereafter the stock turns around and resumes its former upward trend. A professional trader will look for support approximately half way between the support and resistance levels, or at $45. Specifically, $60 less $30 equals $30, times 50 per cent equals $15; $60 less $15 gives an approximate support level of $45.

In reality the sophisticated trader is compromising the one-third, two-thirds retrenchment figures into a 50 per cent guideline. The general rule is noteworthy to the short seller, since it provides a reference point regarding potential repurchase plans. It also enables buyers to select in advance a target area from which a rally is most likely to develop.

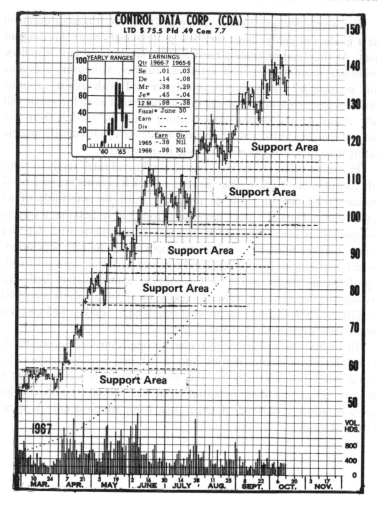

FIGURE 5

The advance in Control Data, which began in early 1967, exemplifies support areas. Bear in mind that support lines are drawn after prices have pulsed out of an existing congestion area.

Chart from *TRENDLINE,* 345 Hudson Street, New York City.

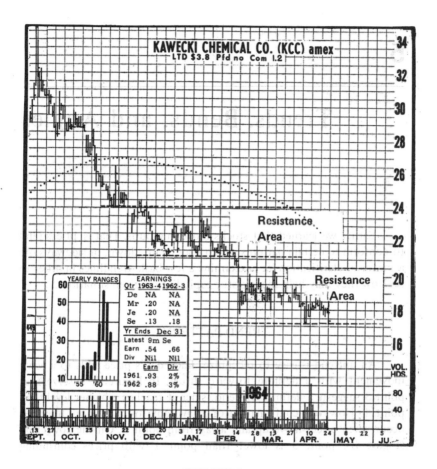

FIGURE 6

Kawecki demonstrates very clear resistance levels beginning with a decline which set in during September. Observe how prices fail to penetrate the resistance line on each major rally except for the slight overlay in early January. A lower resistance area was finally reached in May before recovery established itself.

Chart from *TRENDLINE,* 345 Hudson Street, New York City.

5

Trends, Bends, and Angles

Earlier we learned that stocks move in groups. That is, prices tend to conform to certain patterns which may be up, down, or sideways. As a means of clarification let us examine a few basic trendlines in order to see how they may help the investor capitalize on given situations.

TREND PATTERNS

An uptrend is easy to recognize. Each day's price adds to a wavy movement with a definite forward thrust. In Figure 7, observe that point 3 suggests a definite uptrend, since it reaches a higher level than point 1. However, confirmation of a favorable trend is more likely to occur when prices move up and away from point 3. On the down side (Figure 8), point 3 is lower than point 1 with prices continuing

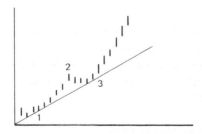 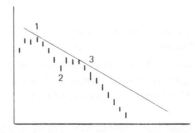

FIGURE 7. UP TRENDLINE   FIGURE 8. DOWN TRENDLINE

downward. It is to be observed that the connecting lines are drawn on the lower or inside part of an upward trend, while the downward trendline is connected at the higher points.

In a sidewise action, the typical price movements appear as in Figure 9. Here, point 1 is on the same level as point 3.

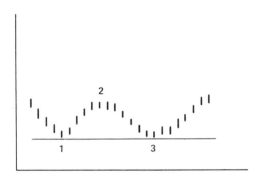

FIGURE 9. SIDEWAYS TRENDLINE

Regardless of an uptrend or downtrend, prices tend to conform to a given in and out limit, or range, which is referred to as a "trend channel." Channels are boundaries in which prices move. The advantage of a channel lies in the simplicity it affords in observing direction and in choosing a buy or sell point. Figure 10 portrays three different channel formations.

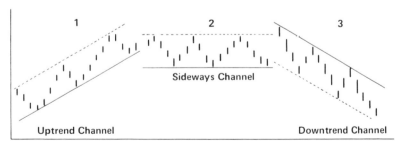

FIGURE 10. CHANNELS

The solid channel line is referred to as the "return line." The dotted parallel line is the directional line, either up, down, or sideways. As a rule, when prices drift down in an uptrend channel and a subsequent rally fails to carry prices back to the return line, it is a sign of technical weakness. A rally from the return line which penetrates the dotted parallel line, either up or down, signals a major breakout to new levels.

The effect of prices swinging back and forth within a trend channel in a step-like pattern is known as "throw back" or "pull back." This pattern is illustrated in Figure 11. The "pull back" offers a second opportunity to minimize losses on the down side or a chance to purchase at a lower price in event of an expected upswing.

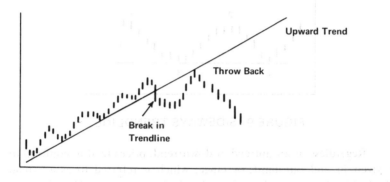

FIGURE 11. THROW-BACK EFFECT

VOLUME DURING TRENDS

Within an over-all trend the volume pattern is important. For an uptrend we should expect increasing volume during advances and decreasing volume during declines. As long as this volume pattern remains intact, we would expect the uptrend to continue, but if volume suddenly increases on a decline, a break in the trendline should be anticipated. The opposite is true during a downtrend. Volume increases on declines, and decreases on rallies. As long as this volume pattern continues, the downtrend can be expected to persist. When a decline is accompanied by decreasing volume, followed by a rally with increasing volume, the over-all downtrend should soon be broken. Observe the volume and trend action in Figure 12.

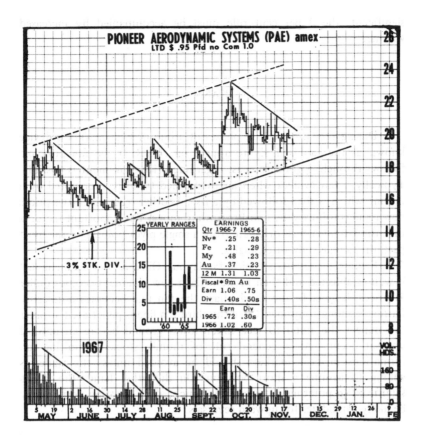

FIGURE 12. VOLUME AND TREND MOVEMENT

Chart from *TRENDLINE,* 345 Hudson Street, New York City.

TREND REVERSALS

Channel situations do not last forever. The technician must look for a signal which will indicate the direction on the next move. As a guide, the accepted position is that a price movement of approximately 3 per cent through the trendline establishes the next trend. Volume is significant; the 3 per cent rule must be accompanied by increased volume.

FANS

During the intermediate phases of a bull or bear market a device known as the fan is likely to appear on charts. If the fan principle follows through, a good forecast regarding price movement is possible. Typically a fan evolves when an established trend is interrupted by a decline which is then followed by a rise. Another reaction carries prices down and is followed by another upward move. The important factor is that the fan lines must originate from a single pivot point. For the most part, the fan has only three angles.

Figure 13 presents a typical fan layout. Observe how each channel is well established and then broken. Each new channel becomes duller as prices decline. In the third phase the fan line becomes noticeably flatter as selling continues. Once the third fan line is penetrated a trader can expect the trend to seek much lower ground before an upward reversal occurs. As a general rule of thumb, stocks exhibiting fan formations in bear markets should be avoided unless the trader is willing to assume a short position. On the other hand, the fan is significant in pointing out securities which, after a resting period, may be likely candidates for upward reversals.

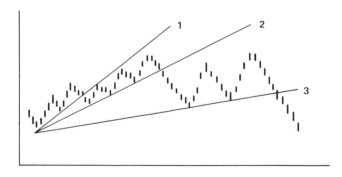

FIGURE 13. FAN LAYOUT

TRIANGLES

Immediately following a broad advance or decline, triangle formations are likely to appear. These are minor pauses, after which the general trend that existed prior to the triangle continues to gain momentum. Several features are evident in Figure 14.

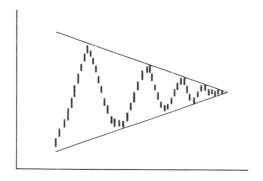

FIGURE 14. TRIANGLE

The obvious action is a coiling process in which fluctuations become smaller and smaller as the apex of the triangle is approached. A simple rule applies to triangles – the coil must thrust prices out of the triangle about three-quarters into it and in the same direction as existed prior to its development. Otherwise a strong reversal pattern is imminent. Experience indicates that prices resume their former direction in a majority of cases.

Triangles may assume any of the following dimensions:

Symmetrical Triangle. By definition this configuration has a balanced arrangement of its parts with prices reacting within the triangle. Commitments should be made after a reliable movement occurs away from the pattern. Volume is most important in confirming the direction of the trend. An upward move requires increased thrust, whereas a downtrend is accepted on little or no increase in volume.

Reversed Symmetrical Triangle (sometimes referred to as a "funnel"). The trader should apply the rules regarding the symmetrical triangle.

Descending Triangle. This represents the most dangerous type of situation, since it denotes a significant bearish attitude, with traders shifting to the selling side. Some buying lifts prices very briefly but the supply is strong enough to penetrate the horizontal boundary line. For example, a quarterly earnings report may have been poor. The stock reacts downward and meets some renewed buying. A few days later the firm may announce a patent infringement suit which shakes trader confidence into renewed selling.

Ascending Triangle. This is the most pleasant situation, since it suggests a move to higher price levels once the overshadowing supply is absorbed. The various types of triangles are compiled in Figure 15.

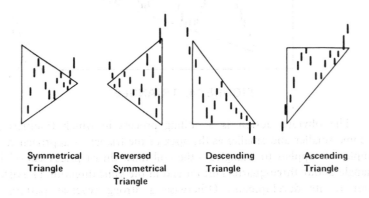

Symmetrical	Reversed	Descending	Ascending
Triangle	Symmetrical	Triangle	Triangle
	Triangle		

FIGURE 15. TYPICAL TRIANGLE FORMATIONS

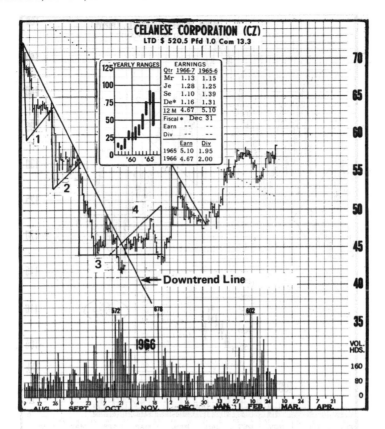

FIGURE 16

Here is an excellent configuration of three triangles resulting from a continuation of the original downturn. Triangles 1 and 2 are symmetrical in form, with each penetration at the apex occurring on high volume. Triangle 3 is a descending type with a major breakout to about $41-3/4. The quick turn to $44 (triangle 4) indicates how treacherous subsequent action may be. On the other hand, since the downtrend line is quite steep, the trader is alerted to the possibility of a quick throw back, as shown under 4.

Chart from *TRENDLINE,* 345 Hudson Street, New York City.

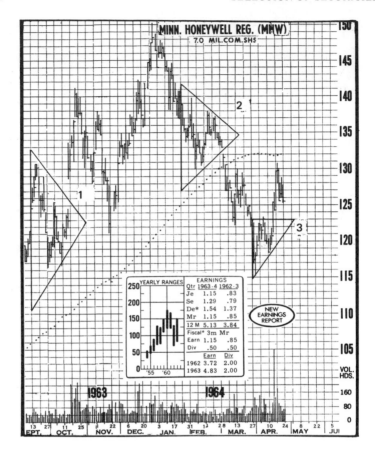

FIGURE 17

Triangles 1 and 2 are symmetrical in nature. Observe the major breakout which occurs in the middle of October. Configuration 2 is another symmetrical triangle which is a continuation of the original downtrend. Pattern 2 is more representative of a symmetrical triangle as it tends to result in a continuation of the original trend. Triangle 3 is a typical ascending type which well rewards the trader.

Chart from *TRENDLINE,* 345 Hudson Street, New York City.

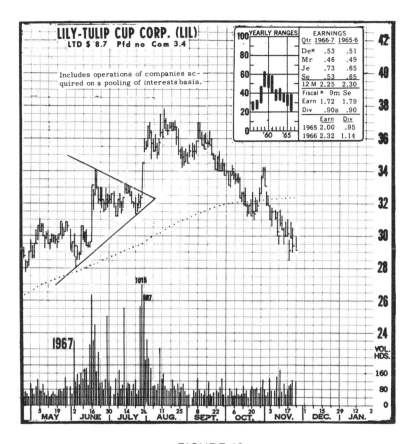

FIGURE 18

Lily-Tulip Cup is a good representative of a symmetrical triangle with all the coiling characteristics. Within a very short period of time the stock rose to almost $38 per share.

Chart from *TRENDLINE,* 345 Hudson Street, New York City.

6

Head and Shoulders Formation

In the previous chapters a variety of patterns were introduced. We now come to a type of formation whose outcome tends to be quite predictable. This pattern is referred to as a "head and shoulders." As shown in Figure 19, it has a remarkable resemblance to the human form.

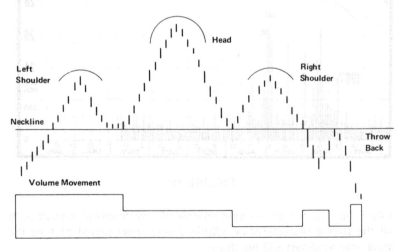

FIGURE 19. HEAD AND SHOULDERS

A closer inspection of the configuration reveals the following stages of development:

Left Shoulder. The shoulder builds up as a result of a strong rally,

30

accompanied by significant volume. Thereafter, a profit-taking reaction occurs which forms the right leg. Volume is noticeably reduced on the downward slope.

Head. Rising prices and increased volume initiate the left leg of the head pattern followed by a contraction, on reduced volume, which extends to the neckline. Observe that the head extends well above the left shoulder.

Right Shoulder. Another price rally produces the left leg of this shoulder and finally the rally breaks up and prices slide downward. Volume action is quite different than in the left shoulder and head formation. More often than not, volume is decidedly smaller than under the left shoulder and head. The right shoulder formation tends to be equal in height with the left shoulder; it is always well below the head.

The unwary trader who unfortunately bought late, usually has an opportunity to redeem himself when a brief minor rally pulls prices back to the neckline. There is no guarantee that such an event will always occur but, as a rule, a continued downtrend is normally followed by a slight recovery. Once the throw back is completed, prices tend to break down into a strong retreat. High volume is apparent in this latter phase, representing an obvious reversal pattern.

The right leg of the right shoulder serves as a significant point of reference to the short seller. For example, when the neckline is penetrated and a throw back occurs, the short seller can effect a short transaction. From the various patterns presented, it can be seen that abrupt downtrends occur which are profitable to short sellers.

Head and shoulders arrangements do not have to rest upon a horizontal plane. Often the neckline may have an upward or downward direction.

IMPORTANCE OF THE RIGHT SHOULDER

Once the right leg of the left shoulder and left leg of the right shoulder develop, a neckline can be drawn upon the chart. At this point, the strength of the right shoulder should be watched very closely. If volume remains very light once the shoulder begins to form a rounded top, then it is obvious that a professional switch or sell is generally warranted. This causes the downward right leg to develop. Once others sense the weakening prices, an orderly retreat develops. Previous stop-loss orders are touched off and the neckline is penetrated. Those on the sidelines observe the reaction and welcome the opportunity to buy the stock at bargain prices. This brings about a minor rally which permits the formerly entrapped traders to supply their shares near the neckline. Finally, the last group of buyers come to realize that the stock is lifeless and scramble to unload their shares for whatever they can fetch. Market psychology is such that a strong reversal is inevitable. The right shoulder invariably signals a big caution to professional traders.

In some instances a false move may occur. That is, in the downward move of the right leg (right shoulder), the price may drift to the neckline and reverse itself in a strong upward channel. This phenomenon is quite rare. The professional should not remain in the stock hoping for this unusual reversal, especially when other opportunities possess greater profit possibilities.

Of basic concern is the extent of the decline once the right leg penetrates the neckline. As a rough guide, a few experts hypothesize that the minimum reversal will equal the distance from the top of the head to the neckline using as a reference point the closing price which broke the neckline. For example, if the distance from the neckline to the top of the head formation involves a rise of 15 points, then the reversal should approximate this number of points, beginning from the closing price which broke the neckline pattern.

This general rule relating to the depth of the decline in a head and shoulders pattern needs to be tempered with other obvious technical conditions surrounding the situation. An alert technician will devote attention to two factors before accepting the rough guides as being absolute:

1.   Prior support and resistance levels
2.   General nature of the market

In many cases, if the prior support level is well below the point indicated by the general rule (distance from the top of the head to the neckline), then the expert technician will accept the latter point as being a more valid indication of the severity of the possible decline. The rationale is that a prior resistance level should be tested to determine if it is a good foundation on which further consolidation can occur before an upward trend develops.

This information is important to both short position traders and those wishing to buy back the stock. The short seller has some indication as to when the stock should be replaced, while the trader who has gone to the sidelines has a similar indication as to when the stock can be repurchased.

Since most head and shoulders formations occur in bull markets, general market conditions become significant in confirming the anticipated action of the pattern. In other words, if the pattern develops near an all-time high for the Dow-Jones Industrial Average, there seems to be a strong tendency to accept it as indicative of a strong impending reversal for the entire market. Thus, a smart trader will be more inclined to go short or sit on the sidelines rather than switch to another stock. On the other hand, if the head and shoulders appears mid-way in the Dow-Jones Industrial Average, chances are that a short position or a switch is in order.

THE INVERTED HEAD AND SHOULDERS

From time to time an inverted head and shoulders may appear. This formation is the opposite of the pattern under discussion. The upside down head and shoulders signals the termination of a downtrend instead of the end to an advancing stage. The relevant factor in this pattern is the nature of the volume. The following points are usually noteworthy in an inverted head and shoulders:

Left Shoulder. A significant downtrend is overcome by a minor rally. As expected, volume is extensive, after which a definite slackening occurs. Thus, the left shoulder is well defined.

Head. A bearish decline forces prices well below the low point of the left shoulder. Volume is generally larger than on the left shoulder. Another strong rally drives prices back to the neckline. On the right leg of the shoulder, volume is noticeably increased.

Right Shoulder. Another reaction, on weak volume, in which the low point fails to extend below the head, is followed by an upward reversal on decidedly increased volume.

If the neckline is penetrated on heavy volume a bullish confirmation is signaled. One should expect a brief pull back to the neckline after which prices should resume their upward momentum. The important element is the break through the neckline on appreciable volume. Absence of volume indicates that the trader is faced with a false move.

The best way to visualize the chart pattern of a head and shoulders is to refer back to the action of our two basic group of traders — buyers (demand) and sellers (supply) — as depicted in Figure 20.

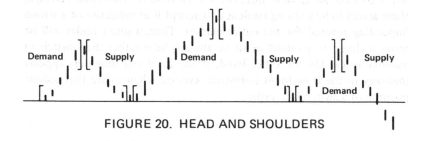

FIGURE 20. HEAD AND SHOULDERS

Left Shoulder. There is obvious demand for the stock from those who accumulated their shares before the upward move along with those who purchased during the uptrend. Near the top some of these traders supply their stock at a profit.

Head. Seeing a technical weakness in a good stock, other traders who were in the stock or on the sidelines use this opportunity to buy. Of course, some who sold on the left shoulder also return to the demand side. But since the supply is limited, in order to accumulate an inventory many traders must pay high prices for a position. Thus, the stock reaches new highs as other supporters, who rely on the penetration of resistance levels on strong volume, move into the situation. Those traders with handsome profits begin to supply the stock and another decline is touched off.

Right Shoulder. By this time the public is well aware of the stock, particularly since it has been making new highs. This group uses this last reaction to get aboard at a seemingly reasonable price. As the stock is accumulated, those wary traders who bought in the upper part of the head area use this vantage point to get out with as small a loss as possible. Consequently the oversupply, contrasted to the small demand, causes the final decline which is strong enough to penetrate the neckline.

The last selling area, the right leg of the right shoulder, represents a conglomerate of traders from the dismembered head and shoulders formation, each of whom shows paper losses on his holdings.

SYMMETRY OF HEAD AND SHOULDERS

The head and shoulders model presented in Figure 19 demonstrates a very neat behavioral pattern. In reality, the symmetry is generally not as rigid. A shoulder may be unbalanced; the head may be pointed or flat rather than curved.

On rare occasions multiple head and shoulders arrangements may appear. Most experts refer to those situations as "complex head and shoulders." Included in this category are formations with two left and two right shoulders, two-headed patterns with the proper number of shoulders, and formations with either two left or two right shoulders. The proliferation of heads or shoulders should not be viewed with alarm. What has been said of the typical model applies also to the hybrid pattern.

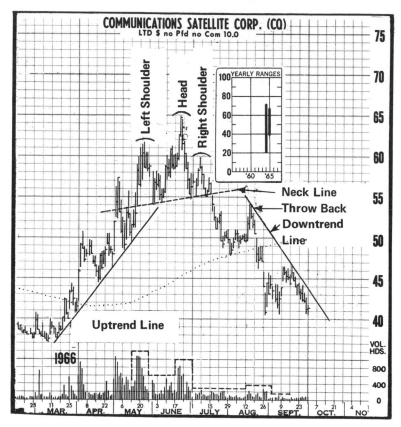

FIGURE 21

Comsat presents one of the clearest head and shoulders arrangements from start to finish. Observe how the volume rises on the left shoulder rally and then contracts on the reaction. On the head, volume is large but not as heavy as under the left shoulder. Volume supports the right shoulder very nicely and then retracts until the throw-back phase is begun. Thereafter, volume resumes a more orderly turnover.

Chart from *TRENDLINE,* 345 Hudson Street, New York City.

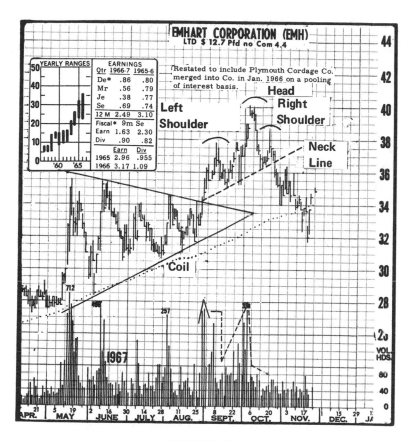

FIGURE 22

Emhart provides an unusually clear and profitable situation. Notice how well the stock snaps upward from a coil situation into a well-formed head and shoulders configuration. Volume lives up to expectations. Observe how the volume increases during declines. In essence the volume predicted an impending upside breakout. Both bulls and bears were well rewarded in this trading situation.

Chart from *TRENDLINE,* 345 Hudson Street, New York City.

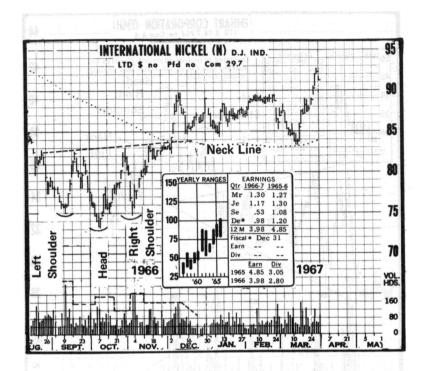

FIGURE 23

International Nickel shows an inverted head and shoulders formation. Observe that the volume movement is especially strong on each shoulder and on the head. The rectangular consolidation pattern which follows the inverted head and shoulders finally breaks out at $90. This upward advance continued to a high of $119 which was reached in December, 1967.

Chart from *TRENDLINE,* 345 Hudson Street, New York City.

7

Wedges, Flags, Rectangles, Pennants

Before embarking upon our next group of patterns let us first introduce a few important technical terms.

From time to time well-established trends are momentarily interrupted. If the trend experiences an imbalance between supply and demand, the shift in direction is referred to as a "reversal pattern." On the other hand, if the price action resumes its former trend the process is known as a "continuation pattern."

WEDGES

Wedges are merely minor patterns which may take one of two forms, falling or rising. In both cases the slope of one boundary is necessarily steeper than the other. For example, in a rising wedge the lower boundary line will be at a steeper angle than the top one. The opposite applies to a falling wedge, as seen in Figure 24.

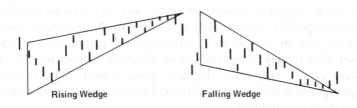

Rising Wedge   Falling Wedge

FIGURE 24. WEDGES

While one might tend to associate a rising wedge with a rising market and a falling wedge with a declining market, in actual practice the opposite holds true. That is, falling wedges are apt to occur in rising markets and rising wedges present themselves in declining markets. Volume action is similar to a triangular pattern; it declines at first and then increases as prices break away from the formation. Buying tactics dictate a measure of success for short selling on a rising wedge, as once prices break out, the decline is swift and quite extensive. Purchase commitments are recommended where falling wedges appear.

FLAGS

Flags are delightful patterns, since their outcome tends to be quite predictable. Basically two types of patterns are discernible, the up flag and the down flag, as seen in Figure 25. Upon closer observation the flag formation resembles a small parallelogram.

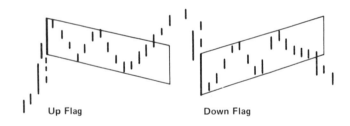

Up Flag   Down Flag

FIGURE 25. FLAGS

The pole of an up flag results from a rapid rise in price and volume, perhaps due to an investment advisory's favorable recommendation. The sudden flurry causes old stockholders, who may have been trapped with the stock in the past, to release their holdings. Thus, the profit-taking action weakens the rally. Prices remain "mixed" in a very narrow channel with each downward quotation being slightly lower than the preceding day's close. Similarly volume slackens. The seesaw activity within the flag lasts about a week. Once the minor supply problem is eliminated, prices and volume suddenly burst upward in a remarkable upthrust.

Down flags are inverted up flags; volume tends to sag within the flag formation and then becomes notably strong as prices break away from the pattern.

RECTANGLES

Rectangles represent a near equilibrium situation. Neither supply nor demand has the upper hand for long periods. Hence, the market price vacillates within a horizontal area for a few weeks or months, as may be observed in Figure 26. Rectangular patterns can usually earn a few points for the quick trader who rides the up and down pattern.

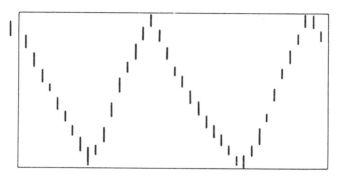

FIGURE 26. RECTANGLE

It is somewhat difficult to tell in which direction prices will break away from the rectangle. Normally, the direction of the breakaway from the rectangle tends to signal the general movement of the stock.

PENNANTS

A relative of the wedge and the flag is the pennant. It may be defined as a pointed flag or compact wedge. Its similarity with the flag is derived from the fact that the pennant has a pole, but thereafter its configuration forms a triangular shape. Notice that the pole of an up pennant slants down in an uptrend and up in a downtrend. (see Figure 27). The volume pattern is akin to the wedge.

MARKET CHARACTERISTICS

The various formations which have been presented are, in effect, consolidation or congestion configurations. This is noticeably true for the rectangle. Flags and pennants are most common in dynamic

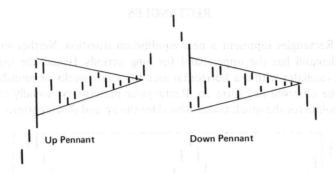

FIGURE 27. PENNANTS

situations. They evolve quite rapidly, within several days, and offer excellent trading opportunities. Up flags and up pennants are most reliable profit patterns. Down flags and down pennants warrant caution in that the design must be extremely accurate. Otherwise a false interpretation may develop. On the other hand, rectangle consolidations are typically found at the bottom of a major decline.

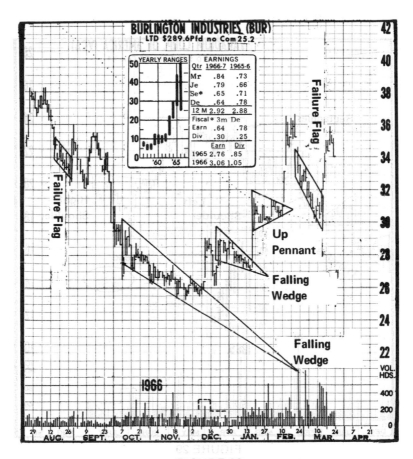

FIGURE 28

The two flag formations are labeled as failure flags because the movements are not valid as in a true up flag. The up pennant is true to form as are the wedge movements.

Chart from *TRENDLINE,* 345 Hudson Street, New York City.

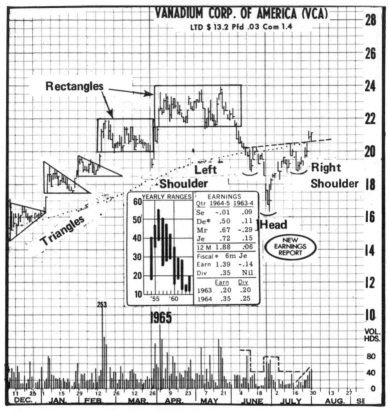

FIGURE 29

A number of incomplete triangles are evidenced in the minor uptrend followed by two rectangles. Note that the breakaway from the top rectangle is a valid trend indication. Thereafter an inverted head and shoulders pattern develops.

Chart from *TRENDLINE,* 345 Hudson Street, New York City.

8

Saucers, Sauce Pans, Bowls, M and W-Triple Tops and Bottoms

SAUCERS

The very terms "saucers," "sauce pans," and "bowls" immediately alert the reader to one common denominator which applies to these three kitchen utensils: namely, curves or a rounding formation. The depth and extent of the rounding determines which term is applied.

Saucers are wide, shallow rounding curves which may be either a bottom or top type of configuration. As seen in Figure 30, prices forming the saucer consist of a series of sideways movements with a very narrow range. The volume pattern is also saucer shaped.

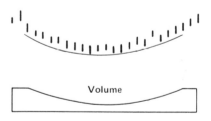

FIGURE 30. SAUCER BOTTOM

These timid saucer formations are most likely to develop among relatively inactive stocks. More often than not, stocks listed on the American Stock Exchange display a saucer pattern. A stock with moves of only a few eighths a day is a likely candidate. Also, a high-grade straight preferred (non-convertible) frequently forms a saucer pattern.

The rationale for the existence of the formation lies in the fact that there is very little reason to buy or sell the stock. Occasionally, a breakaway from the basic pattern will emerge for a few trading days, after which the former trend is resumed. This type of activity must be watched very closely, as a false move may develop. Often, insiders increase their buying, which in turn draws in the public. Finally, news of poor earnings may be announced. By this time the insiders have disposed of their supply and the stock settles down and continues to form a long base. Hence, a short-term trader becomes an involuntary long-term investor.

The most appropriate manner to handle the situation is to:

1. Have a broker's research department check the stock, especially to determine if a quarterly report is forthcoming, if a dividend announcement is due, or if there are other rumors. Note that if the stock involves a callable preferred issue, the unusual market activity may surround the possibility of the firm calling the issue. An obvious *caveat* before committing funds is to check the difference between the current market price and the redemption price of the preferred issue.
2. Have a little patience for a few trading days – at least five.
3. Have your broker purchase a "call" option, preferably of six months' duration.

SAUCE PANS

The proper time for real action is when the saucer formation is nearly completed and the stock begins to form a handle. In this case the saucer is developing into a sauce pan. The connection between the pan and the handle is significant. Frequently, a slight retreat or false downward price move will occur, after which prices will begin to form the handle. In other words, the handle will be not at the top of the pan but a few points below it. Thereafter prices may form a delightful uptrend as seen in Figure 31.

For the most part, saucers require several weeks or three to four months to develop into sauce pans. As one might expect, the inverted sauce pan is a most undesirable situation except to the short seller.

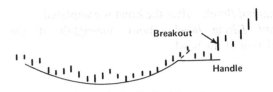

FIGURE 31. SAUCE PAN

BOWLS

Bowls are deeply rounding formations which may be horizontal or tilted as well as inverted (see Figure 32).

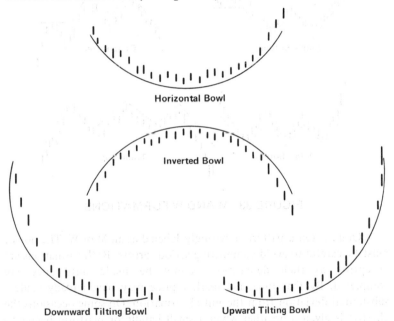

FIGURE 32. BOWL FORMATIONS

The horizontal and upward tilting bowl are bullish types of patterns, whereas the downward tilting bowl is a bearish formation. Most bowls require a month or two to complete. Similarly, volume velocity should conform to a bowl pattern. Buying opportunities present themselves as follows:

1. *Horizontal Bowls* – after the bowl is completed
2. *Upward Tilting Bowl* – about one-eighth of the way from completion of the bowl

M AND W FORMATIONS

The M and W formations are double tops and double bottoms as illustrated in Figure 33.

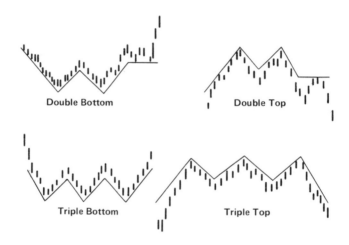

FIGURE 33. M AND W FORMATIONS

Quite often a pattern is wrongly labeled as an M or W. The novice must be careful to avoid committing serious errors. Both formations are deceptive, as their delineation cannot be made until they are completed. By that time, the market price may have already made a substantial deviation from the initial formation. On some occasions the chartist is given a breather when a small handle or platform begins to develop. In these instances the trader can take appropriate action. But more often than not, the handle fails to form and instead a new trend is immediately begun.

Let us clarify the anticipatory market action surrounding M and W patterns. The former configuration, M, is a very bearish situation, while the W is highly bullish. When prices break away from the M, the decline is most severe. A long position in any stock should be liquidated as quickly as possible. The opposite tactic applies to the W formation after the upward right leg is formed.

A closer inspection of the diagrams in Figure 33 reveals that M's and W's reflect market tests of former support and resistance levels. Under the M, resistance rapidly gives way as support withers. However, with the W, support is quite obvious as resistance is overcome. Volume on the two patterns is difficult to forecast. For the most part, the double top is associated with an increase in volume in the areas of the peaks. On occasions volume may be heavy on one peak and light on the other or vice versa. Then, too, volume may be quite light on both peaks. Perhaps the best guide is to look for unusual variations in volume, such as extreme lightness or heaviness and then dullness or the reverse, as a tentative sign of a developing M or W.

It stands to reason that if we can have an M or W, we may also have an extra saw-tooth in either pattern. In such cases a triple top or triple bottom comes into existence. In practice, the triple pattern causes the former M or W to be reversed. That is, the M becomes a W while the W transforms into an M pattern, as shown in Figure 33. Again, the proper time for trading is after the formation is definitely completed.

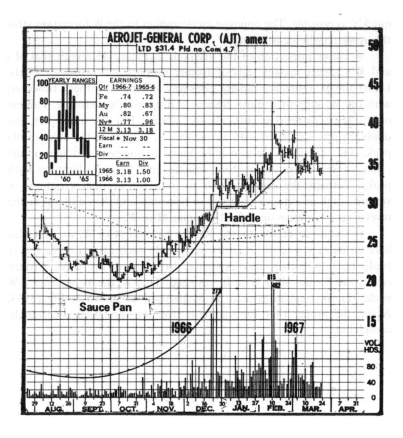

FIGURE 34

Outside of the slight disruption in prices in September, Aerojet forms a good sauce pan configuration. The volume outline, which is well rounded in nature, picks up in December and accelerates on the handle formation. Thereafter turnover remains strong as price pushes upward. Unfortunately, a clear-cut upward pattern failed to develop and the stock settled back from March through October 1967. Notice that the sauce pan is quite deep contrasted to the saucer formation in Brunswick Corporation (Figure 35).

Chart from *TRENDLINE,* 345 Hudson Street, New York City.

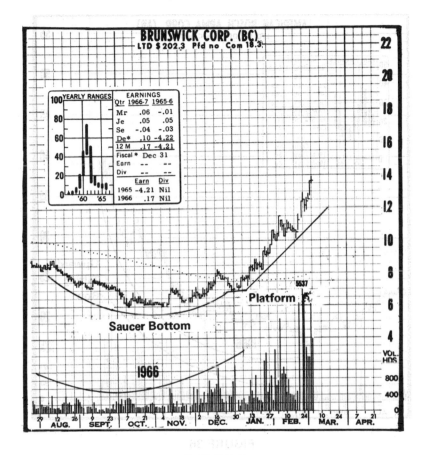

FIGURE 35

Brunswick portrays a typical saucer pattern, with a shallow rounding bottom. Once the handle or platform formed, volume appreciated very rapidly. In turn, prices reacted very favorably in an uptrend move.

Chart from *TRENDLINE,* 345 Hudson Street, New York City.

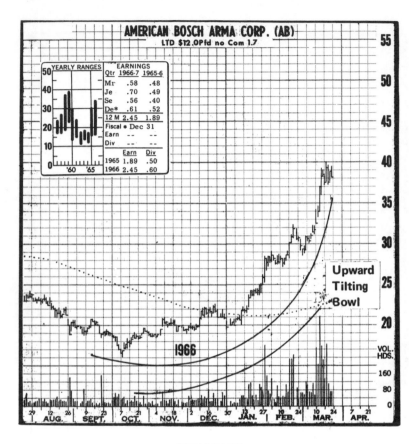

FIGURE 36

This upward tilting bowl pattern in both price and turnover proved to be a very successful holding as prices vaulted to $70 before a slight reaction occurred in October of 1967. An astute chartist may observe the semblance of a saucer formation between September and December; however, the configuration is too uneven for a balanced saucer.

Chart from *TRENDLINE,* 345 Hudson Street, New York City.

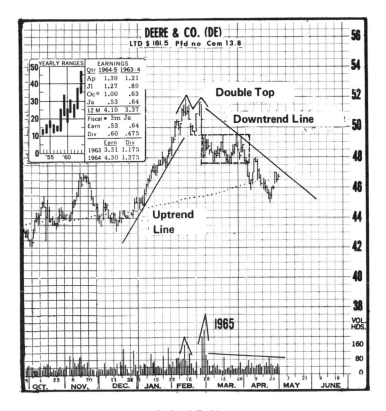

FIGURE 37

Deere portrays a typical double top formation. The first leg of the pattern was built in mid-February on advancing prices which failed to hold in the new area. Another assault, on large volume, toward the end of February brought an increase in the quantity of stock supplied. However, the demand again failed to absorb the supply, since both price and volume subsequently sagged to lower levels. Observe the rectangle digestion area which existed for a month, after which prices retreated into a long decline. In July of 1965, the stock was trading in a $38 to $40 range.

Chart from *TRENDLINE,* 345 Hudson Street, New York City.

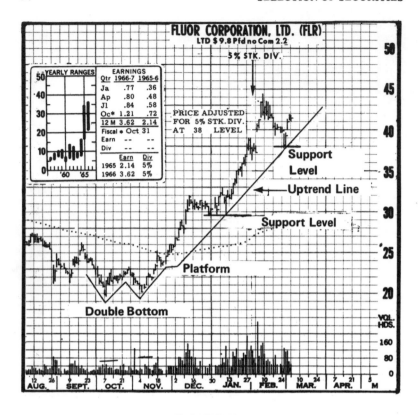

FIGURE 38

Fluor's double bottom is a little unusual in that the first V is formed on light volume; the second V develops in slightly increased turnover. Once the platform is completed, signifying a support area, volume expands with market price, producing a major upward trend. The trader should watch the action of the stock very closely after the stock rises from the second V to determine its ability to rise on larger volume well above the high of the rally occurring between the V's. Until this situation develops the trader should be wary of the possibility that the stock may give way to a triple bottom.

Chart from *TRENDLINE,* 345 Hudson Street, New York City.

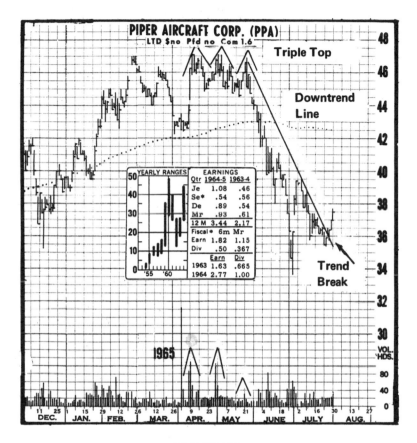

FIGURE 39

This formation contains all the ingredients of a true triple top situation. Each valley is bearishly lower than the prior floor; volume activity on the last top is decidedly smaller. Finally, prices give way in an accelerating decline. A minor recovery does not occur until the trend break in mid-July. Since the reversal is on light volume it is too early to label the situation as a technical correction.

Chart from *TRENDLINE,* 345 Hudson Street, New York City.

9

Gaps and Islands

Gaps are interesting topics for discussion, as there are two different schools of thought regarding their interpretation. One group looks upon them as an evil omen. Another considers them simply as either bullish or bearish indicators depending upon their size and when they appear on the chart. In all instances a certain amount of suspicion is totally warranted. Let us inspect and rationalize the existence of gaps in order to appraise their technical significance.

DEFINITION OF GAPS

We may define a gap as a price range at which no shares are exchanged. For example, a stock may open one day at a price lower than the lowest opening price of the preceding day. Or the stock may open one morning at a price higher than the closing high of the prior trading day. In either event an obvious gap occurs on the chart.

SIGNIFICANCE AND TYPES OF GAPS

The Common Gap tends to occur in a consolidation or symmetrical triangle and in turn reinforces the pattern formation. There is no forecasting significance accruing to such gaps other than the one already noted.

The Breakaway Gap develops after a prominent chart pattern has been formed, and signals the beginning of a major price move. For instance, a move away from a congestion area may be accompanied by a breakaway gap. Normally heavy volume can be anticipated on the advancing move. For example, a stock may be nearing its high for the year. Ordinarily chartists will be willing to buy once the new high has been penetrated. Consequently a large number of buy orders will exist a half a point above the all-time high. By the same token, a large number of buy orders may exist one-quarter below the high from those who may not be willing to pay more for the stock. Once the supply is cleared at the lower price the new buyers will have to pay a half a point more for the stock. Clearly a gap occurs, but such a gap will not appear on the chart, since it occurred during the trading day rather than between trading days. Because a large number of buy orders exist above the all-time high, the accompanying volume will swell to a large number.

More often than not breakaway gaps are conspicuous following overnight news. A firm may announce the receipt of a major contract after the market closes. The next morning a rash of buy orders is likely to bring about a sizable gap. Other developments producing a breakaway gap include such news as a tender offer, merger announcement, significant changes in earnings or dividends, or changes in management, as well as various government actions ranging from an anti-trust suit to contract awards or cancellations. In effect such information falls into two categories, either internal or external in nature.

It is well to observe that gaps may be expected once the neckline of a head and shoulders formation has been penetrated. In addition, a gap is likely to appear when prices move out of a congestion or consolidation pattern.

Runaway gaps manifest themselves during periods of steep, rapid advances or declines. In other words, such gaps are not associated with pattern formations, unlike the two previous types of gaps. The runaway gap will occur well away from any precise configuration.

To some extent the runaway gap is caused by emotional reaction rather than by technical or fundamental factors. For instance, a stock may have had a sharp rise, perhaps resembling an upward tilting bowl. Those who missed the initial opportunity will wait for a reaction. Still others may take a short position because of the sharp run-up. Instead of experiencing a correction, the stock may continue on an upward march. Those who waited for a reaction shift to the buying side, while the nervous short seller, fearing a turn for the worse, attempts to minimize his losses by purchasing the stock. Other buyers observe the volume action, become excited by the advance, and enter the situation. Consequently a wave of demand creates a runaway gap or perhaps a series of runaway gaps.

It should be noted that some technicians prefer to call a runaway gap a "measuring gap," since it tends to occur about half way along a major price move. Thus, a gap may be expected around $70 if a stock has advanced from a $50 support level. In all probability the stock will ascend an additional 18 to 20 points. As a rule a false move is seldom associated with a runaway gap. It is well to remember that in a declining market a runaway gap will probably produce a descent of slightly less than a full one-half. This reference point is particularly important to the strategy of the short seller.

An Exhaustion Gap, as the name implies, appears near the end of a bullish appreciation in a stock. A typical situation indicates little or no resistance in the initial run-up, which approximates a straight line. Then just as suddenly as the stock rose, a large supply overhangs the market, bringing an abrupt halt to the advance, albeit with very heavy volume. The gap makes its presence on or just prior to the last day of the move.

A careful analyst is likely to observe smaller gaps in the early stages of an advance. Such a gap is ordinarily considered as a continuation type. As the advance continues the succeeding gaps should be closely watched for an apparent reversal followed by a congestion pattern. Frequently congestion may set in, after which the price resumes its former trend. The alert trader will want to consider re-entering the situation only after the former upward advance is confirmed; that is, after a clear breakaway from the congestion zone has occurred.

ISLANDS

An island is a small isolated trading zone standing alone on a chart. The island may be composed of a single day's trading or last several days before a breakaway (reversal) is observed.

As a rule, islands are likely to develop after an exhaustion gap is evident. Other things being equal, the island is the end of a formation and a minor reversal pattern tends to establish itself. Traders will want to sell and wait for a new trend to develop before entering the same stock. Beginning with the exhaustion gap and carrying through to the completion of the island, trading volume tends to be highly volatile.

A CLOSING WORD ON GAPS

Many traders believe that gaps must be closed; that is, that on some occasion the price will reach an appropriate level which fills in the missing price. Is such action necessary? No. In all probability the gap will be closed someday. Whether the fill-in takes place in a day, week, month, year, or years hence is immaterial. The typical trader should not concern himself with this matter since, by definition, the technical trader does not plan to buy and hold for an indefinite period of time.

FIGURE 40

The performance of Syntex indicates a remarkable number of gaps as well as extreme variations in intra-day high and lows. The nearly perfectly balanced pattern is akin to a missile poised for take-off. Gaps 1, 2, and 3 are of the runaway type, while 4 is a typical exhaustion situation. Point 5 is a one-day island reversal top. The gap created under 6 represents a breakaway trend followed by a well-developed downtrend fan formation.

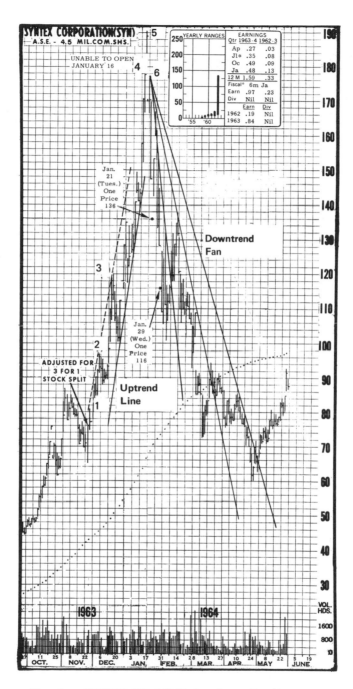

Chart from *TRENDLINE,* 345 Hudson Street, New York City.

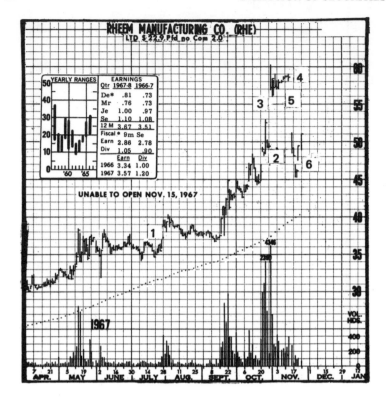

FIGURE 41

From September through late November Rheem presents a series of
gaps or holes resulting from news of numerous acquisitions. The gap
appearing in area 1 is a clear breakaway type from a congestion area. A
deteriorating situation finally filled the gap in August. Gap 2 and 6 are
runaway variations, since they occur in an almost straight-line run-up
and decline. Point 3 is a typical exhaustion gap which signifies a halt to
the rapid move. It is a "blow-off" which brings about the last leap,
which lingers for a brief period. Point 4 is a breakaway gap. The flurry
of activity between 3 and 5 is an island reversal. Notice that it stands
alone and is accompanied by extraordinary trading volume.

Chart from *TRENDLINE,* 345 Hudson Street, New York City.

PART II

Analysis of Point
and Figure Charts

WE NOW MOVE into a different approach to technical analysis — the
point and figure technique, which is the oldest method of chart
forecasting. Long before bar charts were used, insiders, manipulators,
and professionals employed point and figure charts. The method
became available to the public when DeViller published his point and
figure principles.[1] The point and figure method is used less frequently
than the bar chart because it appears mysterious and is therefore
presumably complex. It is not. Once the basic principles and the
mechanics of constructing a chart are understood the technique
becomes remarkably simple. Point and figure differs from the bar
method in that it measures the forces of supply and demand by
graphically depicting the battle between buyers and sellers.

[1] Victor DeViller, *The Point and Figure Method of Anticipating Stock Price
Movements* (New York: Stock Market Publications, 1933).

10

One Point Reversal
Construction

MECHANICS OF CHART CONSTRUCTION

The first step in mastering point and figure is learning to construct the chart. First, arithmetic paper is required. The vertical axis is labeled in a manner similar to the bar chart. But in general each block, rather than each line, will represent one point, as seen in Figure 42.

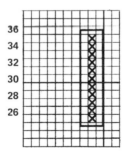

FIGURE 42.

Whenever there is a change in price of one point, an X is placed in the appropriate box. For example, if a stock is selling for $30, and advances to $31, the proper entry is shown as in Figure 43. Although it does not matter what figure is placed in the box, an X is commonly used.

If the price of the stock moves to $33, the entries appear as shown in Figure 44.

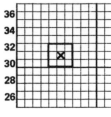

FIGURE 43.

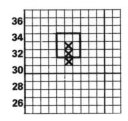

FIGURE 44.

All fractions are ignored. That is, an entry is not made unless the "point" barrier is broken. For instance, if the stock's next move is to $33-7/8, there is no entry. However, if it reaches $34, an entry is indicated as in Figure 45.

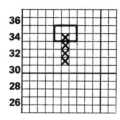

FIGURE 45.

Notice that all entries have been made upward in one vertical column; columns are changed only when there is a change in the price trend. Entries will remain in that column as long as the price continues to rise, whether the advance takes an hour or a year.

Assume that the price of our stock declines to $32. The entries for this move are placed in the vertical column to the right of the column in which the advance was posted, as seen in Figure 46.

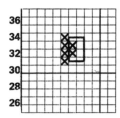

FIGURE 46.

Entries remain in this column as long as the stock continues to decline. If the price of the stock declines further, to $29, the appropriate entries are registered as in Figure 47.

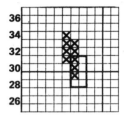

FIGURE 47.

If the price of the stock rises to $30, the X appears as shown in Figure 48.

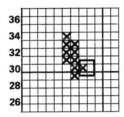

FIGURE 48.

There will never be only a single entry in one column. "When new columns contain only one entry it is a temporary condition; the next price change establishes the direction of that column and must be posted in that column."[2] For example, if the stock moves to $29, the entry is as shown in Figure 49.

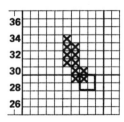

FIGURE 49.

[2] A. H. Whellan, *Study Helps in Point and Figure Technique* (7th ed.: New York: Morgan, Rogers & Roberts, Inc., 1966), p. 6.

This column now records declines in spite of the fact that the preceding entry was on an ascending move. The last two entries should be reviewed again, as they tend to be confusing to the beginner. Let us assume that the stock declines to $26-7/8. The entries are shown in Figure 50.

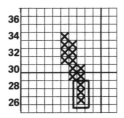

FIGURE 50.

If a rally carries the price to $32, the entries are made as shown in Figure 51.

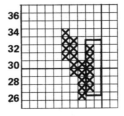

FIGURE 51.

In the foregoing illustrations the classic one point reversal point and figure chart has been demonstrated. The important factors to bear in mind are:

1.   Fractions are ignored
2.   No column has only one entry

VALUE FOR BLOCKS

A question arises as to why each block represents a change of a full point. Why not let each entry represent five points or an eighth of a point? The answer is that a block may represent whatever the chartist desires. The procedure used by the majority of point and figure chartists is to let each block represent one point for stocks with a price ranging from $20 to $100. For stocks selling under $20 each block represents one-half of a point. If the stock is selling above $100, each block may represent one, two, three, or five points, depending on the chartist. The important factor in choosing a definite value is that each block should represent a significant change in the accumulation or distribution of the stock. It is difficult to specify what a significant change may be, but the arbitrary assignment of values to blocks is not a serious hindrance to successful chart interpretation.

A growing number of point and figure chartists are using three point reversal charts in conjunction with their one point reversal charts. Some rely solely upon three point reversal, since these charts require less time to make up and maintain and can be constructed from daily newspaper quotations. A leading proponent of such charts feels that, "They shout where others merely stutter."[3] Although these reasons are commendable, two very crucial points are lost. First, some of the quick short-term gains available with one point reversal are missed, and thus money may be tied up in investments for a longer period of time. Second, an accurate prediction of a projected target price is more difficult to obtain. The three point reversal chart is constructed in the same general manner as the one point, except that there are never less than three X's in any column. If a one point reversal chart is available, a three point reversal chart may be constructed from it by simply ignoring the columns having only two entries. In three point construction each column accurately represents advances or declines, since no columns show both advance and decline moves.

REPRESENTATION OF TIME

Unlike the bar chart, the point and figure chart has no time axis. A point and figure chart indicates accumulation and distribution, buying and selling; it shows the forces of supply and demand in action, not as a relationship of price and time.

To denote time, the usual procedure is to place the first letter of the month or the number of the month in one block in place of an X. The year may be placed at the bottom of the chart. This notation is properly depicted in Figure 52.

[3] A. W. Cohen, *The Chartcraft Method of Point and Figure Trading* (New York: Chartcraft Inc., 1966), p. 6.

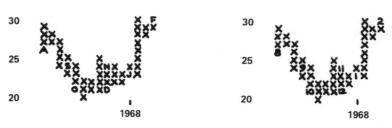

FIGURE 52. U. S. STEEL

DATA FOR CHARTS

The daily newspaper may not provide sufficient financial data for point and figure charts. On slow-moving, low-volume stocks, one can usually determine how a stock moves if the financial section of the paper lists the open, high, low, and closing price.

For the majority of stocks, however, a service is necessary to provide charts and chart data. Such services are especially useful, since they save time in chart construction and also take into account any change in trends occurring during the trading, which would not be apparent in the financial section of a newspaper.

ADJUSTING THE CHART FOR A SPLIT

Stock splits must be taken into account. With a two-for-one split the adjustment involves a new chart; two moves in a vertical column become one move on the new chart. If the split is three for one, every three moves in a vertical column now represent one move on a new chart. Stock dividends of less than 10 per cent may be ignored, but adjustments should be made for any change of 10 per cent or more. A great amount of time may be required to adjust charts to dividends and splits, especially if the split is somewhat unusual, perhaps two for three. Fortunately, any of the chart services will perform the necessary adjustments.

11

The Congestion Area Breakout

DEFINITION OF CONGESTION AREA

What does one look for in a point and figure chart? A majority of the rules pertaining to trendlines and channels which apply to bar charting still hold true, except that greater attention is focused upon the breakout of a congestion area. The congestion area is the point where buyer and sellers do battle. It appears as a lateral cluster of X's, as represented in the examples shown in Figure 53.

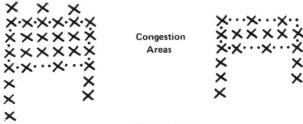

FIGURE 53.

THE BREAKOUT

Most major advances or declines are preceded by a congestion area. A congestion area does not necessarily mean that a reversal is about to begin. A reversal is a possibility but the area could also indicate only an interruption of a trend. A congestion area occurs when the floating supply (those shares available for trading) is increasing or decreasing. If the floating supply is decreasing, an advance eventually follows. On the other hand, if the floating supply is increasing, a decline will take place. Unfortunately only hindsight can be used to judge whether the congestion area represents an increase or decrease in the floating supply. Therefore, the chartist looks for and acts upon a breakout from a congestion area because *the direction of the breakout is the direction of the move.* A model of a congestion breakout, termed by some chartists a "catapult," is seen in Figure 54. Notice how each congestion area is followed by a breakout (catapult) and then a move in the direction of the breakout.

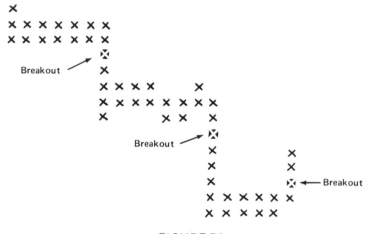

FIGURE 54.

The declines in Figure 55 are preceded by a congestion area. A breakout is not declared until the stock moves past the highest or lowest block in the congestion area.

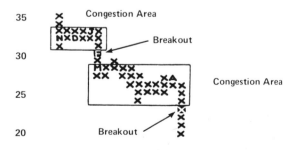

FIGURE 55.   FINANCIAL FEDERAL

The advance or decline which follows a congestion area need not be vertical: there may be some interim movement as seen in Figure 56. Nevertheless, *the direction of the breakout is the direction of the move!*

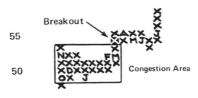

FIGURE 56. MAYTAG

12

Trends

TRENDLINES AND CHANNELS

As with the bar technique, trendlines and channels play a part in point and figure analysis. However, when drawing trendlines and channels in the latter system one cannot be dogmatic. Some slight error is inherent in the arbitrary assignment of values to each block.

When a stock passes $20 or $100, channels and trendlines may become distorted due to the change in the value of the blocks. Remember that common sense and good judgment are important in constructing and interpreting a trendline or a channel.

Figure 57 presents several models of trendlines and channels. You will recall from bar charting that a down trendline is drawn along descending tops while an up trendline is drawn along ascending bottoms.

BREAKING OF TRENDLINE

Trendlines tend to hold very well and are extremely important in both short and long-term analysis; however, the breaking of a trendline does not necessarily represent a reversal. A good example of a stock breaking its trend, going through a period of consolidation, and then continuing its previous trend is seen in Figure 58.

USEFULNESS OF CHANNELS

Channels are rare, but they can be valuable when found. They are especially useful in instances in which there is a sharp vertical penetration out of the channel on the side away from the trendline. An

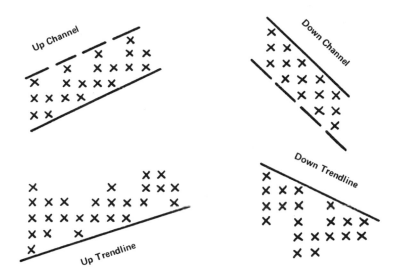

FIGURE 57. TRENDLINES AND CHANNELS

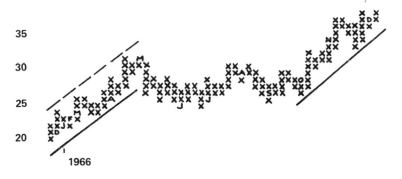

FIGURE 58. METRO-GOLDWYN-MAYER

abnormal vertical advance out of a channel is not an optimistic sign, since it is often an early warning of a pending reversal. This is evident in Figure 59.

The same caution should be used when there is an abnormal decline out of a down channel, as seen in Figure 60 for International Salt. Channels, if wide enough, are useful for trading purposes since they permit the short-term trader to capitalize within a definite trading boundary.

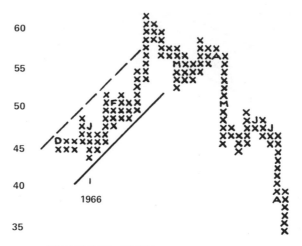

FIGURE 59. PITTSBURGH COKE

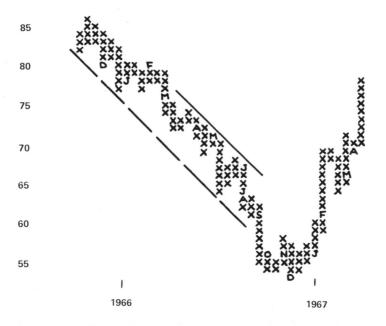

FIGURE 60. INTERNATIONAL SALT

13

Major Reversal Patterns

Obviously, trends do not continue indefinitely. After one has been in progress for some time, certain formations may occur indicating to the point and figure chartist that a major reversal is under way.

THE FULCRUM

The most reliable reversal pattern is the fulcrum. The fulcrum, which is a reversal of a decline, consists of five major phases from the beginning of the configuration to its termination.[1]

1. A Price Decline In the most obvious fulcrum formations, the decline is almost entirely vertical, with little or no lateral movement. In other cases a decline which has some lateral movement may mark the start of a fulcrum. Models of both examples are presented in Figure 61.

FIGURE 61. FULCRUM FORMATIONS

[1] Whellan, *Study Helps in Point and Figure Technique, op. cit.*, p. 21.

2. *Activity Near the Bottom of the Decline.* This is shown in Figure 62.

FIGURE 62.

3. *An Advance* The peak of the advance (Figure 63) should be greater than the height of any of the activity described in phase 2.

FIGURE 63.

4. *Activity at or Near the Bottom of the Fulcrum.* This type of activity is evident in Figure 64.

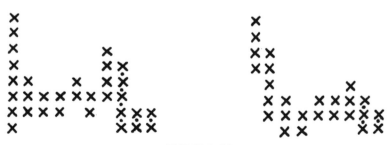

FIGURE 64.

5. *An Upside Breakout.* Once the price passes the peak of the advance in phase 3 a breakout has occurred. The breakout can be

accomplished in a vertical move or it may be accompanied by other
activity, as shown in Figure 65.

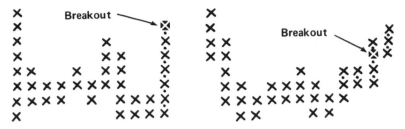

FIGURE 65.

In Figure 66, General Signal forms a fulcrum which signals a major
reversal to the chartist.

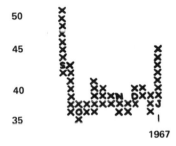

FIGURE 66. GENERAL SIGNAL

Do not become alarmed if the price action in a potential fulcrum
penetrates slightly the bottom or floor. Despite the fact that this is a
slight congestion area breakout, the possibility of a fulcrum should
preclude a short sale. Note in Figure 67 the manner in which Cummins
Engine and Ford Motor penetrate their floors before reversals take
place.

COMPOUND FULCRUM

Every so often a compound fulcrum develops. As might be
expected, this pattern is composed of two or more fulcrums. Ideally,
compound fulcrums tend to have a continuous row of horizontal X's, as
in Figure 68.

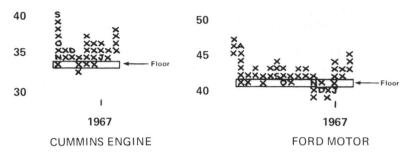

FIGURE 67.

FIGURE 68. DOUBLE FULCRUM

Edison Brothers Stores required approximately three years to form the double fulcrum seen in Figure 69.

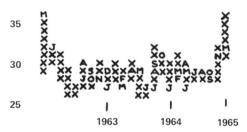

FIGURE 69. EDISON BROS. STORES

INVERSE FULCRUM

An inverse fulcrum signifies the reversal of an advance. It is just the reverse of the fulcrum, having the following major phases:

1.   A price advance
2.   Activity near the top or ceiling

3.   A decline (greater than in any of the activity in phase 2)
4.   More activity at or near the ceiling
5.   A downside breakout

The reversal in Kendall during 1966 meets each of these requirements, as shown in Figure 70.

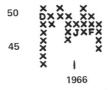

FIGURE 70. KENDALL

THE SAUCER AND INVERTED SAUCER

The saucer and inverted saucer are both signs of a major reversal. As with bar charts, the saucer formations are so labeled because of their rounding characteristics (see Figure 71).

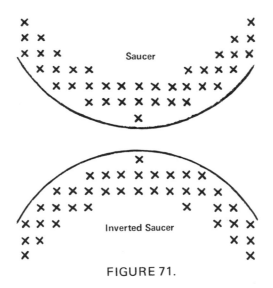

FIGURE 71.

For the most part, saucer tops and bottoms tend to be symmetrical, as illustrated in Figure 72.

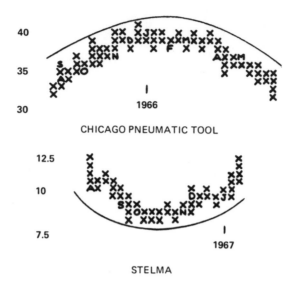

CHICAGO PNEUMATIC TOOL

STELMA

FIGURE 72.

V FORMATIONS

As noted in earlier discussions, many patterns may be formed by channels, trendlines, and congestion a:eas. An abrupt change in a channel may give the appearance of a V or inverted V, as depicted in Figure 73.

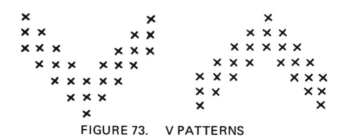

FIGURE 73.   V PATTERNS

Harnischfeger (Figure 74) formed an extremely symmetrical inverted V during 1966.

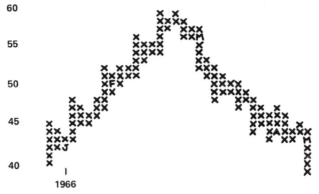

FIGURE 74. HARNISCHFEGER

THE M AND W CONFIGURATION

Several abrupt changes in channels or trendlines cause an M or W to form. These patterns, also referred to as a double top or double bottom, are shown in Figure 75.

Double Top

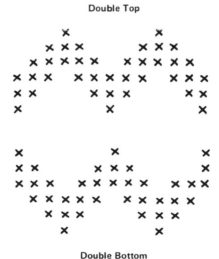

Double Bottom

FIGURE 75.

THE HEAD AND SHOULDERS PATTERN

From time to time a head and shoulders or inverted head and shoulders formation is observable. This is one of the very few formations which may be difficult to interpret as it develops, since the forming of the head initially appears as a continuation pattern rather than as a reversal of a trend. Once formed, however, the head and shoulders or inverted head and shoulders configuration constitutes a major decline. Ideal activity for such formations is seen in Figure 76.

Head and Shoulders

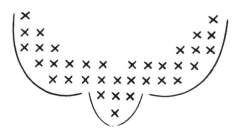

Inverted Head and Shoulders

FIGURE 76. HEAD AND SHOULDERS PATTERNS

It is important that the chartist realize when a major reversal is in progress. Whether the formation is labeled a double top, an M, or a head and shoulders, is arbitrary. For example, the formation in Quaker Oats (Figure 77) could be interpreted as a V or an inverted head and shoulders pattern.

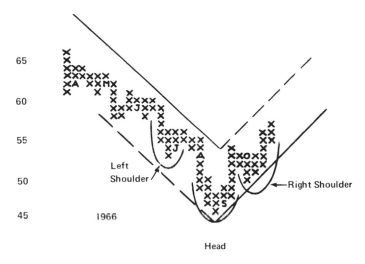

FIGURE 77. QUAKER OATS

14

Miscellaneous Formations

There are other situations which do not necessarily represent major reversals, but which do offer potential profit to the short-term trader.

TRIANGLES

Frequently a congestion area forms a triangle. It may be symmetrical or ascending, usually preceding an advance; or descending, usually before a decline. Various triangular configurations are presented in Figure 78.

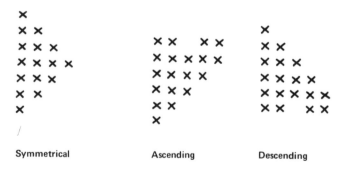

| Symmetrical | Ascending | Descending |

FIGURE 78. TRIANGLES

As with all congestion area analysis, the direction of the breakout is the direction of the move. Crowell Collier formed two triangles in 1966, as shown in Figure 79.

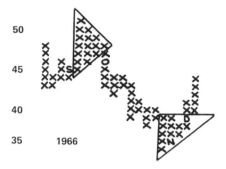

FIGURE 79. CROWELL COLLIER

THE RECTANGLE

The ideal congestion area is a rectangle. This is illustrated in Figure 80. It is ideal because the battle between buyers and sellers takes place between two definite price limits. Notice in Figure 81 the lateral movement between the $28 and $31 boundaries.

FIGURE 80. RECTANGLE

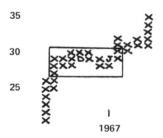

FIGURE 81. WILLIAMS BROS. STORES

THE TECHNICAL CORRECTION

When a stock incurs a rapid vertical move, either ascending or descending, it often develops a pull back (throw back) and then continues its former course of action. This temporary retracement has little lateral movement, and tends to be from one-third to two-thirds of the entire advance. Trans-Lux and Emery Air Freight illustrate the throw back effect in Figure 82.

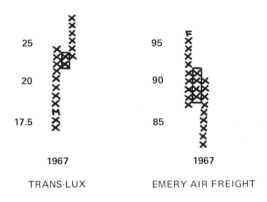

FIGURE 82.

15

Support and Resistance

IMPORTANCE OF THE CONGESTION AREA

It is to be recalled that support and resistance are key factors in bar charting; they are equally important in point and figure. The congestion area acts as support or resistance, depending upon whether the stock is advancing or declining. Old resistance levels become new support and vice versa.[1] A stock may encounter resistance during a climb, but once the congestion is passed, the previous resistance becomes the new support level as seen in Figure 83.

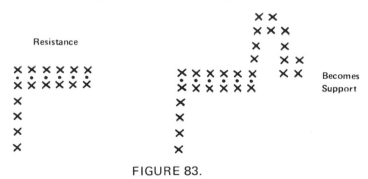

FIGURE 83.

Similarly, a stock may incur support during a decline. However, once overcome, the support area becomes a resistance level (see Figure 84).

When a stock is rising and confronts a resistance area, it usually appears to penetrate the resistance level slightly, move laterally, and then either advance to the next resistance level or decline to the next

[1] The reader is urged to review the logic behind support and resistance in Chapter 4.

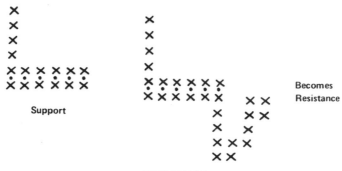

FIGURE 84.

support level. The stock may not actually penetrate the support area, but due to the arbitrary assignment of values greater than one-eighth of a point to the blocks on the vertical axis, the chart appears to have its resistance areas immediately penetrated.

In general the same analysis applies to a declining situation. If a stock moves down to an area of support, it may slightly penetrate the support level, have some lateral fluctuations, and either decline to a lower support level or advance back to the next resistance level.

Seldom will a stock rip through a resistance level in a vertical fashion. However, during panic periods stocks may penetrate potential support levels as easily as a rock falling through a spider web. When the news of President Kennedy's assassination was released, there was an unprecedented decline in almost every issue.

DETERMINING SUPPORT AND RESISTANCE LEVELS

One method of determining how much resistance or support a stock might meet is reflected in the following example:

1. The price of a stock is $36 and an advance is expected. In order to establish resistance and support levels, focus attention on all the activity since the last major reversal (see Figure 85).
2. Turn the page 90° until the price axis lies along the bottom.
3. Allow the X's to "fall" to the axis, as in Figure 86.
4. Turn the page back to its original position.

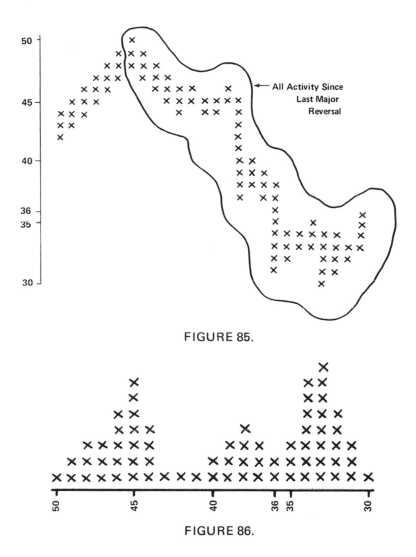

FIGURE 85.

FIGURE 86.

The price ranges which occur most frequently during the decline signify
the resistance area. Recall that the present price of the stock is $36.
The $33 to $34 area provides support. Some resistance may be
encountered at the $37 to $39 range. Strong resistance should be
anticipated in the $44 to $46 area, as graphed in Figure 87.

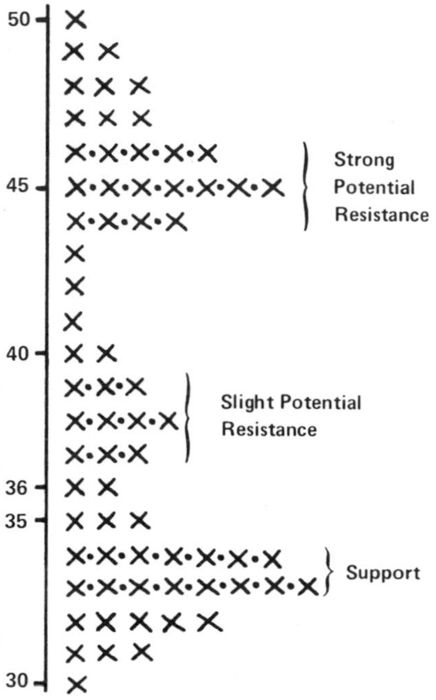

FIGURE 87.

A better approach, albeit more time consuming, is to consider all
the X's for the past several years and apply the preceding four steps to
determine potential support and resistance areas. This approach is
recommended because support and resistance do not depend entirely
on recent activity.

The process of determining support and resistance areas should be
done mentally before taking a position. The degree of lateral activity
that a stock may have during an advance or decline depends upon
support and resistance.

EXPLANATION FOR SYMMETRY

Support and resistance analysis explains why the character of such
formations as saucers, V's, and others is symmetrical. This may be
illustrated by an example. In Figure 88, LTV Aerospace has broken a
downtrend and has almost completed a fulcrum. If a breakout occurs in
the upward direction, what should be expected? To determine where

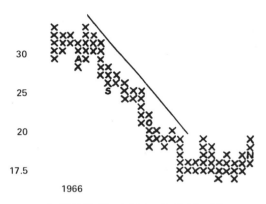

FIGURE 88. LTV AEROSPACE

some lateral movement should be anticipated, draw in the potential resistance zones as in Figure 89.

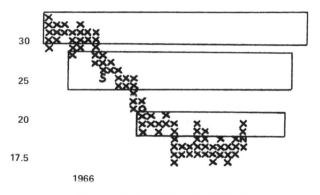

FIGURE 89. LTV AEROSPACE

Ideally the degree of lateral activity on an advance should be the same as that encountered during the decline. In the case of LTV (Figure 90), the sideways movement on the rise is similar to that of the decline until the $27 mark is reached.

AREAS VOID OF SUPPORT AND RESISTANCE

Spectacular moves are frequently observed in stocks that have surpassed their record highs or descended below their record lows. The

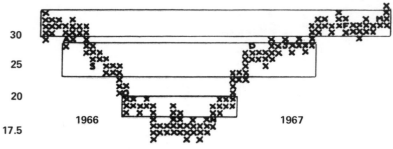

FIGURE 90. LTV AEROSPACE

reason for such activity rests on the fact that no prior resistance or support exists to cushion the move. When stocks are in these areas the only cushion existing is the hope developed among traders, which, more often than not, fails to materialize.

16

The Projected Target Price

AN ELABORATION ON CONGESTION AREA ANALYSIS

Assuming that a congestion area precedes an advance, the lateral movement within a given price range represents a decreasing supply for trading purposes. Conversely, if congestion occurs before a decline it indicates an expansionary trend in the available supply surrounding a given price range. The price move which follows a congestion area tends to be directly proportional to the width of the congestion area. It is significant to note that projected target prices based on the congestion area can be expected to reach their objective about 70 to 80 per cent of the time.

MECHANICS OF FINDING THE TARGET PRICE

The mechanics of finding target prices for obvious congestion areas are simple. Assume that there is a breakout from a rectangular congestion area. To determine how much of an advance is expected:

1. Find the row of continuous (or nearly continuous) X's which is closest to the floor (the floor being the lowest horizontal row in the congestion formation). See Figure 91.
2. Count the number of X's in this row. Include blank spaces if the row is nearly continuous; in the example there are nine.
3. Starting from the X which is on the extreme right of the continuous row, count upward the number of X's obtained in step 2. Include the starting X in the count. (This process may also be

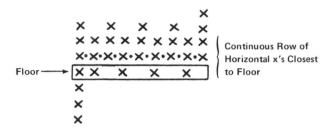

FIGURE 91.

accomplished by swinging a compass the length of the continuous
row, using for a pivot the X which is on the extreme right of the
continuous row.) The target price is presented in Figure 92.

FIGURE 92.

The advance should carry at least to the indicated target price
before a reversal occurs. The advance may or may not be vertical,
depending on the degree of resistance encountered.

The same target analysis holds for a downside breakout:

1. Find the row of continuous (or nearly continuous) X's which is
    closest to the ceiling (the ceiling is the uppermost row of a
    congestion area).
2. Count the number of X's in this row. Again include any blank
    spaces if the row is not continuous.
3. Starting from the X which is on the right end of the continuous

row, count down the number obtained in step 2. Figure 93 presents this approach.

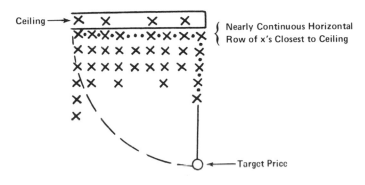

FIGURE 93.

The general rule for finding the target price for all congestion area breakouts is as follows:

1. Find the row of continuous (or nearly continuous) horizontal X's which touches the congestion area walls (a wall being a vertical column of X's which bounds the congestion area), and is furthest away from the breakout, as seen in Figure 94.

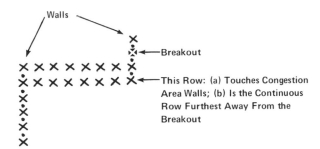

FIGURE 94.

2. Count the number of X's in this row, including blank spaces.
3. Apply the amount obtained in step 2 in the direction of the breakout. Remember to use the X which is on the right of the continuous row as the starting point.

The target price need not be reached in a vertical fashion. Western

Union's decline to its target price was nearly unhampered by lateral movement, as shown in Figure 95. But notice the extent of the activity which transpired before the target price of the advance was reached (Figure 96).

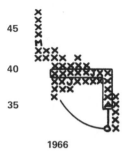

FIGURE 95. WESTERN UNION

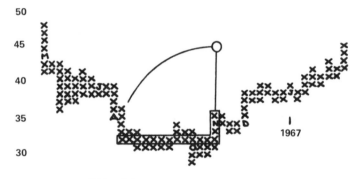

FIGURE 96. WESTERN UNION

After a breakout has occurred, each target price should be reached before the stock makes a reversal and returns to penetrate the congestion area. Unfortunately the length of time required for a stock to reach its target price cannot be predicted with the point and figure method, since time loses its significance on the chart.

FULCRUM TARGET PRICE

Fulcrum target prices are established (in the case of an advance) by finding the row of continuous or nearly continuous horizontal X's closest to the floor and counting upward the number of X's in the row (see Figure 97). As with every target price, use the X on the extreme right of the horizontal row as the starting X in the count. The analysis remains the same for an inverse fulcrum, except that the row of horizontal X's closest to the ceiling is used for the downward count.

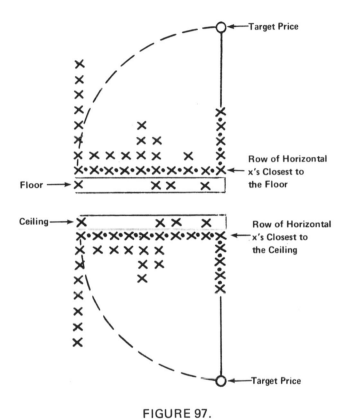

FIGURE 97.

After a target price is reached in a fulcrum, a congestion area tends to build up from which a breakout in the direction away from the fulcrum should be expected.

OTHER TARGET PROJECTIONS

As long as walls are present on both sides of the congestion area it is relatively simple to determine target prices. However, when walls are not present, as in a V or saucer pattern, target prices are not as easily predicted. Usually V's, saucers, head and shoulders, M's, and W's indicate that a major reversal with broad implications has taken place. Some guidelines are presented in the next few pages for obtaining target prices for major reversals, but bear in mind that the target price set by these guidelines is long range and should be regarded as an objective that may be approached but not always reached.

To find the target price for a V, first find the horizontal row which is in the middle of the V. Second, count the number of X's that are in this row (including blank spaces in the count). Third, apply the number obtained in the second step upward. Remember to use the X which is on the extreme right of the horizontal row as the first X in the upward count. Figure 98 properly illustrates the target price for a V.

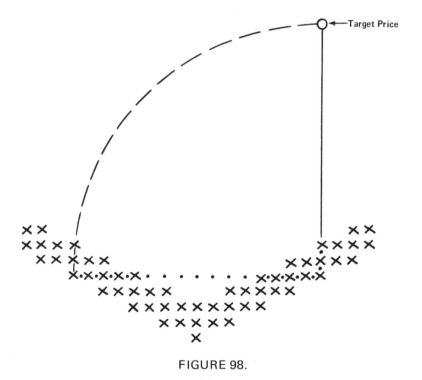

FIGURE 98.

A W is rare, but when it is formed, its target price is projected by finding the horizontal row which bisects the W, counting the number of X's in this row (as usual, include the blank spaces), and counting upward. The correct procedure for obtaining the target price for a W is illustrated in Figure 99.

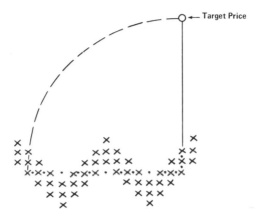

FIGURE 99.

In actual practice a pattern is seldom as symmetrical as in Figure 99. Figure 100 shows how Boeing formed a W and continued upward to fulfill a price objective of $72.

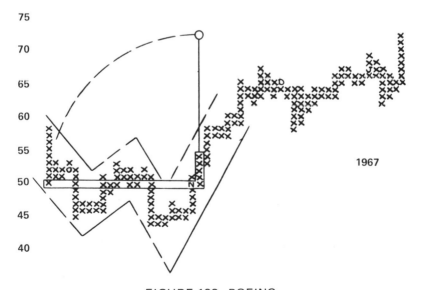

FIGURE 100. BOEING

With the saucer, count the X's (blank spaces included) in the horizontal row in the middle, and apply this amount upward as in Figure 101.

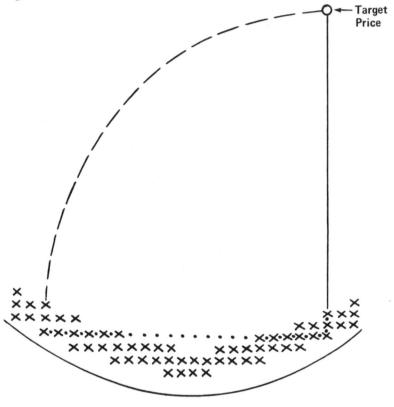

FIGURE 101.

Apply the number of X's (and blanks) in the row which forms the neckline of an inverted head and shoulders in an upward direction to obtain the target price (see Figure 102).

The same general rules apply when obtaining price objectives for an uptrend reversal. Figure 103 illustrates several models and the method for achieving their target prices.

As previously mentioned in Chapter 13, saucers tend to be symmetrical. Therefore the middle row of this pattern is used to obtain the target price. American Shipbuilding (Figure 104) exemplifies the relative ease of determining the middle row and target price of an

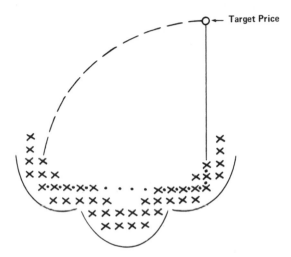

FIGURE 102.

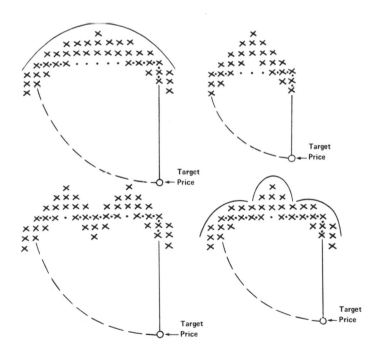

FIGURE 103.

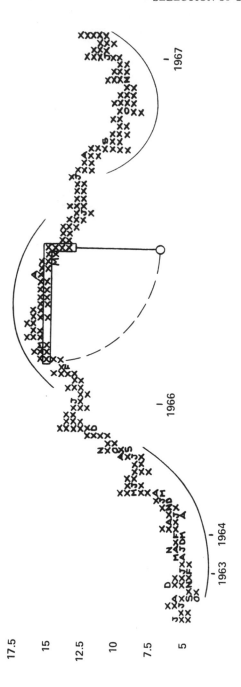

FIGURE 104. AMERICAN SHIPBUILDING

inverted saucer. But even though the projection was easily performed, it proved inaccurate, since a reversal took place before the target price of $7 1/2 was reached. Hindsight reveals that if the nearly continuous row at $16 had been used, the target price of $9 would have been obtained.

Other major reversals are not usually quite as symmetrical as the saucer. Therefore two different chartists may obtain two different middle rows from which to project their respective target prices. The obvious discrepancy cannot be eliminated, since interpretations vary from person to person.

THE BROAD CONGESTION AREA

At times the chartist will observe the building of an extremely broad rectangle. In such cases immediate, intermediate, and long-term price objectives may be projected. The chartist employs the most continuous horizontal row of X's available and applies it in the direction of the breakout. The immediate target price is not difficult to obtain, since there tends to be a completely continuous or nearly continuous row of X's with which to work. The intermediate and long-term price objectives may be found by utilizing different sections of the horizontal row of X's. The particular section chosen depends upon the chartist's interpretation of the congestion area. Although long-term price objectives may be determined, a word of caution is in order. The entire congestion area should not be judged solely as accumulation (a decrease in the floating supply) or distribution (an increase in the floating supply). It is usually a combination of accumulation and distribution. Any long-term projection of prices should therefore be regarded with appropriate suspicion. Figure 105 presents an interpretation of the different price objectives obtained for a very broad congestion area of TRW.[1]

Target prices may also be obtained for triangular congestion areas. Figure 106 shows how symmetrical triangle target prices are projected: that is, by using the number of X's in the horizontal row which bisects the triangle and applying it in the direction of the breakout. For ascending triangles, use the number of X's in the most continuous row

[1] Allan R. Shaw, "Interpretations on the Technical Side," *The Wall Street Transcript*, April 17, 1967, p. 9770.

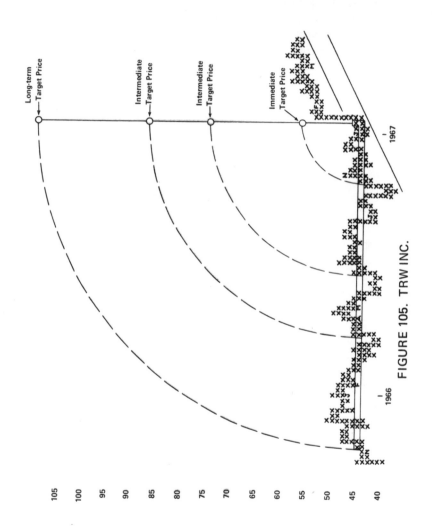

FIGURE 105. TRW INC.

FIGURE 106.

nearest to the breakout if the breakout is for an advance (see Figure 107). If there is a downside breakout, the same row is used to determine the downside target price. Likewise, as shown in Figure 108, the descending triangle will use the number of X's in the continuous row nearest the breakout, if the breakout is headed for a decline. If an upside breakout occurs, the same row is used.

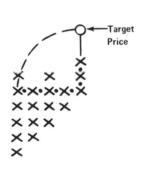

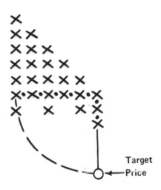

FIGURE 107.   FIGURE 108.

ADJUSTING THE TARGET PRICES

Whenever a target price crosses the $20 or $100 mark, it must be adjusted to take into consideration the change in values of the blocks. For example, Figure 109 shows United Aircraft's target price to be 8 points above $96. Swinging a compass gives a false target price of $108, 12 points above $96. The target price is adjusted by realizing that each block above $100 is worth twice as much as those below. Eight points above $96 gives a target price of $104, as seen in Figure 109.

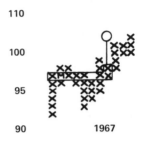

FIGURE 109. UNITED AIRCRAFT

17

Technical Indicators
of the Stock Market

The purpose of this chapter is to bring together a number of factors which influence the direction of the stock market and stock prices. The more important elements that provide basic data for judging whether the technical position of the market is strong or weak include:

1. Advance-decline indices
2. Short interest
3. Odd-lot Theory
4. Confidence Index
5. Customer credit balances
6. Relative strength

ADVANCE-DECLINE INDICES

A valuable guide to market strength or weakness is evidenced in the advance-decline index which appears daily in the *Wall Street Journal* on the inside of the last page under the heading, "Market Diary." The daily data give the breadth of activity for the latest trading day plus a few earlier days for comparative purposes. The information refers to the number of issues traded, and the proportions of that total that rose, declined, or remained unchanged for that day. Also included is the number of listed New York Stock Exchange stocks that made new highs or lows for the year on that particular day.

Using the "Market Diary" coupled with the Dow-Jones Industrial

Average, analysts are able to project the near-term movement of the market. The following principles apply to any given set of facts:

1. When the number of issues advancing exceeds the number of issues declining and the Dow-Jones Industrial Average is rising, the over-all market movement is upward. In other words, the market is "technically" strong.

2. When the number of issues advancing exceeds the number of issues declining and the Dow-Jones Industrial Average is declining, the downward movement in the Dow-Jones Industrial Average will be reversed within a short period of time.

3. When the number of issues declining exceeds those advancing and the Dow-Jones Industrial Average is falling, the decline is reinforced and further declines will occur. That is, the market is "technically" weak.

4. When the number of issues traded on the down side outnumber those rising while the Dow-Jones Industrial Average is rising, a reversal in the Dow-Jones Average is imminent.

The logic relating to the above set of principles is quite simple. The breadth index pertains to the market as a whole, whereas the Dow-Jones Industrial Average relates to a few selected stocks.[1] For a few days the Dow-Jones Industrial Average may move counter to the advance-decline index, but it will have to change in order to comply with the majority of stocks in a declining phase. In essence, the movements of non-Dow-Jones stocks are more pervasive of market action and thus influence the Dow-Jones composition.

A well-known author, Joseph E. Granville, has designed an advance-decline line to measure the underlying strength of the market.[2] The mechanics of Granville's index are simple and quite worthy of attention.

A technician develops an advance-decline indicator by adding the number of stocks that advance and decline on a daily basis, and then subtracting the smaller figure from the larger to obtain a "cumulative differential." The cumulative differential is then plotted to produce the advance-decline line (see Table 2).

[1] For an elaboration of the breadth index, see Paul L. Dysart, Jr., "Bear Market Signal," *Barron's,* September 4, 1967, pp. 9-12.
[2] Joseph E. Granville, *A Strategy of Daily Stock Market Timing for Maximum Profit* (Englewood Cliffs, N. J.: Prentice-Hall, Inc., 1960), pp. 125-134.

TABLE 2

ADVANCE-DECLINE INDEX

Date	Advance	Decline	Cumulative Advance	Cumulative Decline	Cumulative Differential
10-19-67	682	566	682	566	+ 116
10-20-67	465	786	1147	1352	− 205
10-21-67	650	605	1797	1957	− 160

SHORT INTEREST

Just as we have investors who buy a stock in hopes that it will appreciate in value, so do we find those who are pessimistic regarding certain stocks. These latter traders employ the technique of short selling in order to make a profit upon an impending decline in the price of a stock.

Short selling involves the immediate selling of stock which is borrowed from a brokerage house in expectation that the price will decline. If a price decline occurs, the short seller profits by purchasing an equivalent number of shares of the same stock at a lower price to return to the brokerage house. The difference between the selling price and the later repurchase price represents the gross profit to the short seller. If a sufficient number of individuals have sold a particular stock short, a potential demand is created which will tend to support the issue and add additional upward momentum for a rally.

A large published short interest signifies a technically strong market, since a substantial latent demand is created by short sellers who must eventually replace those shares already sold.[3] This can be a

[3]For a brief contrary study of short interest data, see Barton M. Biggs, "The Short Interest — A False Proverb," *Financial Analysts Journal*, July-August, 1966, pp. 111-116.

significant factor in an upward swing. At such times the short sellers panic and become anxious to close out their commitments. Obviously the additional buying action on the part of the short seller acts to propel prices sharply upward. Conversely, a declining or small short interest position for an individual stock or the market as a whole indicates a technically weak situation, since substantial buying power is removed from the market.

The short interest position for the New York Stock Exchange and American Stock Exchange is published a few days after the 15th of the month in leading financial papers, such as the *Wall Street Journal* and *Barron's*.[4]

From the published short interest table the short interest ratio may be calculated for use as a technical indicator of market strength. The ratio indicates the average number of potential trading days represented by the short position. It is the ratio of the reported monthly short position to the average daily volume for that particular month. That is, if the short interest is 6,000,000 shares and the average daily volume is 9,000,000 shares, the short interest ratio is 6.67. As a rule, whenever the ratio rises above 1 it indicates a technically strong market.[5] A particularly bullish situation exists if the ratio exceeds 2.[6] A technically weak position is evident when the ratio is below 1. It is of interest to note that *Barron's* compiles a short interest ratio under its "New York Stock Exchange Monthly Figures."

ODD-LOT THEORY

Of all the market barometers designed for forecasting, none has come under so much criticism as the Odd-Lot Theory. The theory maintains that the general public tends to mistime trades by selling

[4] According to the Research Department of the New York Stock Exchange, the short interest is reportable to the Exchange as of the 15th of the month. If the 15th is not a trading day, the reporting date is the Friday prior to the 15th. The short interest is released to the public after the close of the NYSE on the 3rd market day. The filing of this data is a NYSE requirement for its members.

[5] Bear in mind that the short interest includes "selling against the box." This technique is used mainly for tax purposes by investors who have paper profits but wish to delay the tax until the following year. In practice the investor will sell short the same stock he owns, thus hedging against a price decline. Normally selling against the box increases in December with the stockholder covering the short with his own stock after the New Year. Hence, profits are carried over to the next year.

[6] "Is Short Selling Bullish or Bearish," *Business Week,* December 3, 1966, p. 130.

when prices are rising and then changing to the buying side when market prices are about to decline.[7] At this juncture the sophisticated trader can profit by following a contrary path of action.

By definition, odd lots are transactions involving anywhere from 1 to 99 shares. Such transactions are traditionally carried out by smaller, less informed investors with small amounts of capital.

Historically the theory is measured in one of two different ways: (1) the on-balance approach, or (2) the odd-lot ratio method. The on-balance method, which is more commonly followed, is determined by taking the difference between customer purchases and the combined total sales, which consists of customer short sales plus other sales. Table 3 presents a typical example.

TABLE 3

ON-BALANCE METHOD

Date	Customer Purchases	Short Sales	Other Sales	Total Sales	On-Balance Figure
October 5, 1967	470,596	6,001	496,089	502,090	31,494

Clearly, the on-balance figure indicates that odd-lotters are net sellers for that particular day.[8] As long as odd-lot net sales exceed customer net purchases, the market is technically strong. If the odd-lot on-balance figure favors customer purchases, then a bearish signal predominates professional thinking.

The odd-lot ratio is found by taking the combined total of odd-lot customer purchases plus total sales divided by the reported New York Stock Exchange round-lot volume. For example, on October 11, 1967, the *Wall Street Journal* reported the data shown in Table 4 relative to the odd-lot ratio.

[7]For an elaboration of the original odd-lot theory, see Garfield A. Drew, *New Methods for Profit in the Stock Market* (Boston: The Metcalf Press, 1955).
[8]The *Wall Street Journal* carries the "Odd-Lot Trading" transactions as reported by Carlisle & Jacquelin and DeCoppet & Doremus. Similar information appears on a weekly basis in the "Market Laboratory" section of *Barron's.*

TABLE 4

ODD-LOT TRADING

Date	Customer Purchases	Short Sales	Other Sales	Total Sales
October 9, 1967	686,133	6,276	713,046	719,322

Since the New York Stock Exchange volume was 12,000,000 shares, the odd-lot rates can be determined as follows:

$$\frac{686{,}133 + 719{,}322}{12{,}000{,}000} = \text{about } 11.7 \text{ per cent}$$

Any significant increase in the odd-lot ratio should be regarded with suspicion, as chances are that the public is buying near the end of a bull market.[9] A ratio of 20 per cent has been the average over the past 46 years.[10]

Ever since Garfield Drew introduced the Odd-Lot Theory, its validity has been questioned.[11] Recent skeptics explain that the small investor is more knowledgeable than 10 or 20 years ago. Also, the former odd-lotter has found a safer haven in mutual funds rather than acting for his own account.[12] A statistical study by Kewley and Stevenson, while somewhat limited in scope, suggests that the Odd-Lot-Theory is meaningless in terms of predictive value.[13] While

[9]For a question and answer discussion on odd-lots, see "What Now Little Man?," *Barron's,* July 3, 1967, pp. 1, 3, 12.
[10]The 20 percent ratio was quoted by Mr. Sander Landfield, partner of Carlisle & Jacquelin, in a personal note.
[11]Drew, *op. cit.,* pp. 196-199;
[12]Victor J. Hillery, "Wall Street Debates Wisdom of Performance of the Small Investor," *Wall Street Journal,* September 29, 1966, pp. 1, 14.
[13]Thomas J. Kewley and Richard A. Stevenson, "The Odd-Lot Theory as Revealed by Purchase and Sale Statistics for Individual Stocks, "*Financial Analysts Journal,* September-October, 1967, pp. 103-106. See rejoinder to above article by Garfield A. Drew, "A Clarification of the Odd-Lot Theory," *Ibid.,* pp. 107-108. Also, see, Joseph J. Seneca, "Short Interest: Bearish or Bullish," *The Journal of Finance,* March, 1967, pp. 67-70.

the credibility of the theory is open to controversy, it is sufficient to remember that many traders rely upon it as an important signal in conjunction with other indices.

CONFIDENCE INDEX

An indicator with a remarkable degree of forecasting accuracy is the Confidence Index computed and published by *Barron's*. The governing principle of this index is that sophisticated investors reflect the degree of their business confidence in the economic outlook by their action in the bond market. The theory asserts that when bond investors are optimistic regarding business prospects they invest in high-yielding bonds. By definition such bonds have a large degree of risk or exposure to loss. However, when the economic outlook appears pessimistic, the intelligent bond investor seeks refuge in the higest-grade bonds which, of course, yield a smaller rate of interest.[14]

The movement between low-yielding (high-grade) bonds and high-yielding (lower-grade) bonds indicates the confidence in the economy. Basically, the index is a ratio of the yield on 10 high-grade corporate bonds to the average yield on 40 Dow-Jones bonds.[15]

When the Confidence Index rises, the general indication is that there is a movement into lower-quality (high-yielding) bonds. Market technicians interpret this as a signal to purchase stocks. Conversely, when the index falters, traders construe this as a bearish sign and stocks are liquidated. Also, short selling begins to increase in this period.

Past performance of the index reveals that it is an intermediate type of market indicator. That is, it tends to lead predicted movements in the stock market from two to four months. It is important to remember that a very small change in the Confidence Index is insignificant. In the event the index gives close signals – one down, one up, and then down again – the latter signal resolves the general direction of the trend.

---

[14]For an interesting discussion of the past success of the Confidence Index, see Joseph E. Granville, "Market Forecaster?," *Barron's*, September 7, 1959, pp. 9, 20.

[15]The formula for computing the index is as follows:

$$\frac{\text{Yield on 10 high-grade bonds}}{\text{Yield on 40 Dow-Jones bonds}} = \text{Confidence Index}$$

CUSTOMER CREDIT BALANCES

Customer credit balances are simply dollar amounts of uninvested funds left on deposit with brokerage firms. Such balances are derived from selling securities without an off-setting purchase. It represents money temporarily left on deposit by those on the sidelines. Normally credit balances are associated with sophisticated investors and traders.

The status of credit balances may be found in the *Federal Reserve Bulletin* under the heading of "Stock Market Credit." Other leading financial papers reprint the data. Historical evidence tends to indicate that credit balances increase during the early part of a rising market. However, as the market nears its top, credit balances are drawn down as reinvestment takes place. It is also interesting to note that the decline in credit balances tends to end a little before the troughs of stock market price declines. Thus, credit balances serve as a good technical indicator of both bull and bear markets.[16]

MOVING AVERAGE INDEX

A number of technicians and advisory services employ a moving average approach to trend analysis. The purpose of using this computation is to cancel out the high and low values in a series in order to determine the direction of an individual stock or the market in general. The major advantages to moving averages as measures of a trend are: (1) to eliminate the projection of a trend on the basis of personal judgment; (2) to remain within the framework of the data being plotted.[17]

Typically, most veteran analysts compute a 200-day moving average or some variation thereof.[18] The mechanics involve adding up the closing price of the Dow-Jones Industrial Averages for 200 consecutive days and then dividing by 200 to arrive at the base figure. On the following day the first number of the 200 days is dropped and

---

[16]For an interesting set of principles relating credit balances to the Dow-Jones Industrial Average, see Sloan J. Wilson, *The Speculator and the Stock Market* (Palisades Park, N. J.: Investors Library, Inc., 1963), pp. 10-11.

[17]William A. Spurr, Lester S. Kellog, and John H. Smith, *Statistics* (Homewood, Ill.: Richard D. Irwin, Inc., 1955), p. 333.

[18]See, for example, "Daily Basis Stock Charts," *Trendline* (New York: Trendline Division of Standard & Poor's Corporation).

the new Dow-Jones Industrial Average for that day is added to the bottom of the column. (For clarification review the five-day moving average for the Dow-Jones Industrial group shown in Table 5.) The average is then plotted on the bar chart along with the changing daily price quotation for the stock.

TABLE 5

MOVING AVERAGE INDEX

Day	DJI Average	5-Day Moving Average	Moving Average
(1)	(2)	(3)	(4) (Col. 3-4)
1	800		
2	802		
3	805		
4	808		
5	811	4026 (total of days 1-5)	805.2
6	816	4042 (total of days 2-6)	808.4

Joseph E. Granville has established the following rules as a guide to interpreting the superimposition:

1. If the 200-day average line flattens out following a previous decline, or is advancing, and the price of the stock penetrates that average line on the upside, the action comprises a major buying signal.
2. If the price of the stock falls below the 200-day moving average price line while the average line is still rising, this event also is considered to be a buying opportunity.
3. If the stock price is above the 200-day line and is declining toward that line, fails to go through and starts to turn up again, this occurence is a buying signal.
4. If the stock price falls too fast under the declining 200-day average

line, it is entitled to an advance back toward the average line and the stock can be bought for this short-term technical rise.

5. If the 200-day average line flattens out following a previous rise, or is declining, and the price of a stock penetrates that line on the downside, this action comprises a major selling signal.

6. If the price of the stock rises above the 200-day moving average price line while the average line is still falling, the action is also considered to be a selling opportunity.

7. If the stock price is below the 200-day line and is advancing toward that line, fails to go through and starts to turn down again, the event is a selling signal.

8. If the stock price advances too fast above the advancing 200-day average line, it is entitled to a reaction back toward the average line and the stock can be sold for this short-term technical reaction.[19]

Since the moving average irons out extreme price fluctuations, it may well be that a trend reversal will show first in the price of the stock and then in the moving average. In such situations the best alternative clue is in the volume action of the stock. If the decline is on large volume, other things being equal, it is advisable to sell the stock.

RELATIVE STRENGTH

Veteran chartists frequently wish to know how their stock is performing in relation to other stocks or to some other index. The tool for comparing individual stock prices either to an index of the market or to an industry group is the relative strength indicator. The mechanics for developing an appropriate measuring device are not too difficult to assemble.

One simple method is to compare the closing price of a stock with the Dow-Jones Industrial Average. For the sake of simplicity, assume

[19] Granville *op. cit.,* pp. 237-238.

that the closing price is $60 and that the Dow-Jones Industrial Average closed at 1200. The following procedure applies:

1. Divide the closing price of the stock by the Dow-Jones Industrial Average.

$$\frac{\$60}{1200} = 0.05$$

2. Multiply the result by 1000 or some other convenient multiple in order that the result may be easily plotted.

$$0.05 \times 1000 = 50$$

3. Enter the figure on a separate chart at the resulting level.

The interpretation of the relative strength chart is made by relating the most current entry to the previous entries. As long as the trend is upward, the stock is outperforming the Dow-Jones Industrial Averages. Conversely, as long as the trend is downward, the stock is not performing as well as the Dow-Jones Industrial group.

While relative strength charts are plotted using the Dow-Jones Industrial Average, some analysts prefer to base the calculation on Standard & Poor's 425 Industrial Stock Price Index or 500 Composite Price Index. In addition, the forecasting might also include a comparison of a specific stock to a particular Standard & Poor's industry group. The necessary historical data are found in Standard & Poor's *Security Price Index Record,* and current information appears in the weekly *Outlook.*[20]

We have by no means exhausted the list of indicators which may serve to interpret the technical strength and weakness of the stock market or a particular stock. There are many other theories, both plausible and questionable.[21] For example, the GM Theory holds that if GM makes a new high or low within four months of its previous high or low it indicates the trend for the market. GM does have a significant impact on the economy and must be regarded as a "bell-weather" stock.[22] However, it is equally obvious that no single statistical method is

[20]For a good example of relative strength employing S & P's procedure, see Jerome B. Cohen and Edward D. Zinbarg, *Investment Analysis and Portfolio Management* (Homewood, Ill.: Richard D. Irwin, Inc., 1967), pp. 516-517.

[21]See, for example, Charles J. Colins, "Effect of Sunspot Activity on the Stock Market," *Financial Analysts Journal,* November-December, 1965, pp. 45-56.

[22]Robert H. Stovall, "Directional Signal," *Barron's,* October 27, 1969, pp. 9, 14.

totally dependable. The technician must learn to employ several indicators to increase the reliability of his prognostications, and hence his success in the market. It is this eclectic approach by which leading advisory services project the technical strength and weakness of the market.[23]

[23]See, for example, *The Dines Letter,* October 6, 1967, (New York: James Dines & Co., Inc.), p. 5.

18

Selection of Stocks
for Charting

How many stocks should a person chart? A quick reply is "no more than can be prudently handled within an allotted time period." A good rule is not to watch every stock. It is impossible for one person to exercise careful judgment concerning a large number of stocks, and such judgment should not be sacrificed for the sake of quantity. As a general guide remember that firms fall into well-defined categories, such as railroads, steels, drugs, and the like. Thus, one or two firms exhibiting the characteristics of an industry can be chosen for charting. One difficulty for the young chartist is in the area of conglomerates (multi-diversified firms). For purposes of simplicity, one should chart these firms on an individual basis rather than attempting to classify them into a specific industry. In very recent years, conglomerates have shown some tendency to perform as a group. That is, an upward movement in Ling-Temco-Vought has brought a similar response in Litton Industries and the other corporate conglomerates.

AREAS OF STOCK PREFERENCE

A good guide in selecting specific chart candidates is to watch their volume performance. One must be careful, since a few hundred shares traded in a closely held situation may represent a large turnover relative to the available supply.

Firms listed on the New York Stock Exchange and American Stock Exchange must meet minimum listing requirements. However, the minimum number of shares publicly held and minimum number of stockholders (of round lots) is much larger for the New York Stock

Exchange than for the American Stock Exchange. Consequently, much more erratic patterns may develop in trading securities listed on the American Stock Exchange. As a general rule, avoid very low-price stocks.

A most desirable starting point for selecting chart candidates is the short interest position tables published monthly in leading financial newspapers. The key is to select those stocks with a rising short interest. In theory those stocks with a rising short interest must be replaced, since in effect a "call" is placed on the stock at a lower price. Since the short interest is advancing, the market cannot possibly satisfy all the short sellers at a lower price. Thus many traders must replace the stock at a higher price. Hence, a rising short interest position becomes a bullish factor. In reality, the supply available at a lower price has a greater demand than can be accommodated. The short seller thus can command the stock only at higher prices. In addition, as the price of the stock begins to rise an interesting buying scramble develops as short sellers attempt to minimize their losses. It follows then that a prudent trader will avoid joining the short selling line when the short position is increasing.

Another interesting area to search for chart prospects is the *Official Summary of Security Transactions and Holdings* compiled by the Securities and Exchange Commission.[1] This monthly publication relates information regarding purchases and sales of securities by officers, directors and others having "inside" status.

The significance of inside transactions has been refined by Perry F. Wysong in his market service, "Consensus of Insiders." Wysong uses several official summaries to construct an index (consensus) of the strength or weakness of insiders' transactions. While the service is relatively new, Mr. Wysong's record in locating profitable situations, especially for the chartist, is quite remarkable.[2]

A few of the leading investment advisory services compile a list of stocks recommended by the various advisory services.[3] The caution flag applies here, as the chart performance may indicate that some of the

[1]United States Securities and Exchange Commission, *Official Summary of Security Transactions and Holdings* (Washington: U. S. Government Printing Office).
[2]Carl J. Loomis, "A New Inside Track," *Fortune,* December, 1967, pp. 216-217.
[3]See, for example, *United Business and Investment Report,* October 9, 1967, p. 410. It is interesting to note that *Trendline* service has a special section devoted to "Selected High Volume-Velocity Stocks."

stocks are near their peak and should be avoided. Nevertheless, this appears to be a very fruitful source of stocks for chart action.

"THIN" ISSUES

In recent years there has been a remarkable shift in emphasis to "thin" situations. A "thin" situation is one characterized by few shares of issued common stock, generally less than a million. Moreover, in such issues, a large portion of the available supply is closely held by management. Naturally, the price action of these issues can react quite violently. A typical case is Cameo-Parkway Records, which moved from a little less than $2 1/8 in the early part of 1967 to $55 by September. Approximately 56 per cent of Cameo's 620,000 shares is closely held, which leaves a floating supply of about 273,000 shares. Needless to say, every trader likes a fast mover; however, a thin issue can also plunge rapidly in response to a minimal amount of selling. The most sensible protection a chartist can use in such circumstances is the "stop order."[4]

[4]For a discussion of "stop orders" see Wilford J. Eiteman, Charles A. Dice and David K. Eitman, *The Stock Market* (4th ed.: New York: McGraw-Hill Book Company, 1966), pp. 130-133.

19

Generalities Pertaining
to Charting

TACTICAL COMMENTS

Chart analysts and meteorologist have one thing in common: They both wish to avoid false predictions. As a means of minimizing the possibility of a false move the chartist should ask himself the following questions:

1. Does the chart have a favorable formation? If it does, then it will attract others. Avoid a position in a stock that fails to possess desirable patterns.
2. Does a trendline have to be broken? A long-term position should be avoided if a trendline must be broken in order to complete a pattern.
3. Does the stock chart well? A brief historical review helps to determine if the stock is susceptible to false moves. There are some stocks, although few in number, that do not lend themselves to chart analysis.
4. Does the market move in the direction of projected forecasts? Go long in bull markets and short in bear markets.

A FINAL OBSERVATION

From a philosophical point of view the chartist must learn to develop "market poise." By this we mean a sense of confidence in a trading venture which has been made only after careful and deliberate chart analysis. Moreover, when a mistake has been made, he must retrace the steps and determine whether the proper signals were there but were misinterpreted. It is extremely easy to undervalue some important clue.

While the fundamental goal of stock market followers is to find a method which predicts stock market price movements with a high degree of accuracy, it must be remembered that the underlying purpose of technical analysis is to help the individual trader obtain an edge over other investors in the market place. Whether the chartist prefers bar charting to the point and figure method is immaterial. The main point is to discover, through experience, that method which proves most profitable over a period of time. Moreover, the trader can reinforce the effectiveness of his chart interpretation and hence his performance by combining the use of such technical indicators as short interest, relative strength, and the like (discussed in Chapter 17) into his analysis.

Text Cross- References

	TEXT CHAPTERS				
	Amling	Bowyer	Clendenin and Christy	Cohen and Zinbarg	Dougall
PART I	17, 19				
and/or		10, 20			
			10		
PART II				3, 13, 14	
					20
of this book may be used to supplement the following chapters.					

Eiteman, Dice and Eiteman	Hayes	Leffler and Farwell	Prime	Sauvain	Vaughn
20,21,22,23					
	Between Sections III & IV or IV & V				
		32, 34			
			8		
				17, 18	
					18,19,20,21

Index